Kanyen'
Tewatati
(Let's Speak Mohawk)

by

David Kanatawakhon Maracle
University of Western Ontario, London

 An Audio Cassette Program

Specially created to accompany this
book are 3 instructional audio-cassettes.
They are available from the publisher.

Guilford, Connecticut

Developed at the Centre for the Research and Teaching
of Canadian Native Languages, University of Western
Ontario, London, Ontario, Canada

KANYEN'KEHA TEWATATI
LET'S SPEAK MOHAWK

ISBN: 0-88432-706-X Text and audio cassettes
ISBN: 0-88432-723-X Text only

Published by Audio-Forum,
a division of Jeffrey Norton Publishers, Inc.,
On-the-Green, Guilford, CT 06437

KANYEN'KEHA   TEWATATI
(Let's Speak Mohawk)

This audio-cassette/book program is designed to help the learner acquire correct pronunciation and essential grammatical structures for speaking Mohawk. It is the feeling of the author of this program that the sooner a student is introduced to and learns to manipulate certain aspects of Mohawk grammar, the sooner she or he will be able to acquire conversational use of the language.

Accompanying this program are cassette tapes providing pronunciation of all of the Mohawk language used in this program.

The Mohawk used throughout this program is written using the Standard script (orthography). The Standard form presents the language in a clean and aesthetic fashion making use of diacritics only when grammatically necessary. Each Mohawk entry is provided with a pronunciation key (in syllable form) that should prove helpful in the initial stages of Mohawk acquisition.

It is my sincerest hope that those using this program will gain enough knowledge of the Mohawk language to be encouraged toward eventual fluency.

David Maracle
Kanatawakhon

CONTENTS

* * * * * * * * *

THE SOUNDS OF MOHAWK

The Mohawk language, as represented by this writing system, makes use of twelve (12) letters (a, e, h, i, k, n, o, r, s, t, w, y) and one symbol used to represent the glottal -'-, a sound also considered to be a consonant. In some other writing systems, the letter i is used in place of the y. These twelve letters are used to represent the 6 vowels and 10 consonant sounds found in the language. Learning to pronounce the sounds correctly and efficiently will require a certain amount of practice, especially the nasal vowels, -on- and -en-, the consonant -r-, the aspirate -h-, and the glottal represented by the apostrophe -'-.

Oral Vowels

Vowel	Mohawk	Pronunciation	English	Notes
a	ahta	[áh-ta']	shoe	like a in 'father'
e	wàke'	[wà:-ke']	I'm going	like e in 'they'
	kàsere'	[kà:-se-re']	car	like e in 'met'
i	ise	[í:-se']	you	like ee in 'see'
o	ohsera	[óh-se-ra']	year	like o in 'note'

Nasal Vowels

Vowel	Mohawk	Pronunciation	English	Notes
en	owenna	[o-wén:-na']	word	like u in 'sun'
on	ohonhsa	[o-hónh-sa']	ear	like oo in 'soon'

Semi-Vowels

The following two letters, considered to be consonants in the English language are often referred to semi-vowels in Mohawk, that is, *w* and *y* may act as consonants when between vowels or another consonant and a vowel but will occur as vowels *o* and *i* when occurring between two consonants.

Letter	Mohawk	Pronunciation	English	Notes
w	*owira*	[o-wí:-ra']	baby	like *w* in 'wind'
y	*oyana*	[o-yá:-na']	pair	like *y* in 'yes'

Consonants

Mohawk uses only five consonants in its writing system. The pronunciation of these consonants will require some practice in associating the letter with the sound.

Letter	Mohawk	Pronunciation	English	Notes
k	*kàsere'*	[kà:-se-re']	car	like *g* in 'gate'
	wakthare	[wák-tha-re']	I'm speaking	like *k* in 'speak'
t	*tare'*	[tá:-re']	He' coming	like *d* in 'dog'
	katstha'	[káts-tha']	I use	like *t* in 'take'
n	*onen*	[ó:-nen']	now	like *n* in 'now'
r	*raksa'a*	[rak-sá:'-ah]	boy	like *r* in 'run'
s	*ohsera*	[óh-se-ra']	year	like *s* in 'sun'
	kàsere'	[kà:-se-re']	car	like *z* in 'zoo'

ASPIRATES and GLOTTALS

These two sounds are very important in the Mohawk language. The are considered to be consonants and their inclusion or exclusion in words can, in some cases, have a very dramatic or embarassing effect on what the person may have said. Both of these sounds will require a fair amount of practice on the part of the person learning the language. Since both sounds do not occur in the English language as accepted sounds, it is often very hard for the English speakers to actually hear the difference between the two. However, for a native speaker of the Mohawk language, these two sounds come through loud and clear.

ASPIRATE: The consonant -h- has two uses in expressing the written language. It may occur a consonant such as *h* in hat, or as an aspirate occuring as a small puff of air at the end of a syllable or before a consonant. Proper acquisition of this sound will require a fair amount practice for most students. The best approach is to have a native speaker say words containg aspirates very slowly, to listen carefully, and then to mimick the pronunciation as closely as possible. Use the following words for practice.

ahta [áh-ta']   shoe(s)
ohwihsta [oh-wîhs-ta']   money
ohsnonhsa [oh-snónh-sa']   hand / finger

Don't get discouraged, because though acquiring this sound may take a while, once you've got it you'll have it for good.

GLOTTAL: The apostrophe is used in this particular writing system to designate the glottal. This sound does not occur in Standard English but does show up in many of its dialects. It sounds very close to the first -h- in the English expression "oh-oh". Again, as with the aspirate, the best approach is to listen to a native speaker and mimick the pronunciation of words containing glottals. Use the following words for practice.

o'tàra [o'-tà:-ra']   clay
a'nowara [a'-nó:-wa-ra']   turtle
ka'nahkwa [ka'-náh-kwa']   barrel

It may take a while to get on to but once you've acquired it you will hear it popping up everywhere (even in the way some people speak English).

<u>NOTE</u>: In this particular spelling system the glottal -'- is not often written when it occurs at the ends of nouns, however it will occur in most cases at the ends of verbs and within all words where it may occur.

VOWEL and CONSONANT COMBINATIONS

VOWEL COMBINATIONS: There are also two additional vowel sounds, diphthongs (double vowels), that occur in Mohawk. In the past these vowels would probably have consisted of two syllables, possibly separated by consonant *h* or glottal '. In time the consonant was dropped and the two vowels came to be sounded as one.

> *ae*   sounds like -i- in b<u>i</u>te.
>
>> *aetewahninon'*   [<u>ae</u>-te-wah-ní:-non']
>> *You & I should buy it.*
>
> *aon*   sounds like -ou- in s<u>ou</u>nd with a slight nasal quality.
>
>> *aonsakahtenti'*   [<u>a-on</u>-sa-kah-tén:-ti']
>> *I should go home.*

CONSONANT COMBINATIONS: There are also combinations of consonants that also occur in Mohawk. Below are listed the more commonly occurring combinations. Some have no English equivalent, however the following will attempt to give as close a pronunciation as possible.

> *kw*   is pronounced with the *k* sounded as *g* in <u>g</u>ate, and the *w* as in <u>w</u>ay.
>
>> *Takwahrori*   [ta-kwah-ró:-ri]
>> *Tell me!*

ty   is pronounced with *t* sounded as *d* in <u>d</u>ate, and *y* as in <u>y</u>et.

To i tyahtenti [to i tyah-tén:-ti]
Let's you & I go home

sy   is pronounced as *sh* in <u>sh</u>eep before vowels.

ohsyàkara [oh-<u>shi</u>-à:-ka-ra']
waist

<u>Note</u>: In the Tyendinaga Mohawk Dialect the consonant-vowel syllable *si*
is always pronounced as <u>she</u>.

th   is pronounced similar to the *t* in <u>t</u>ake with the h of the
combination being pronounced: ie. *tha* sounds like <u>t-ha</u>.

kataweyàtha' [ka-ta-we-yà:-<u>t-ha</u>']
I enter a place

kh   is pronounced similar to the *k* in <u>k</u>ick, however in nearly all
instances the h of the combination is pronounced: ie. *khe*
sounds like <u>k-hay</u>.

wa'khehrori' [wa'-<u>k-hay</u>-hró:-ri']
I told her / them

sh   is pronounced similar to the *s* in <u>s</u>ee, however in nearly all
instances the -h- of the combination in pronounced: ie. *she*
sounds like <u>s-hay</u>.

shehrori [s-hay-hró:-ri]
Tell her/ them!

(7)

tsy   has a pronunciation that is midway between the sound *j* in jar and the *ch* in <u>ch</u>urch.

otsitsya   [o-tsì:-tsya']

PRONUNCIATION GUIDE

The Mohawk provided in this book will occur in two forms. The form occurring in bold script (Standard Orthography) provides an efficient and easily recognizeable presentation of the word. The form given inside the brackets [ ] provides a syllable presentation of the word useful in recognizing the actual sound divisions in the language. This pronunciation guide should prove useful in learning the pronunciation of the word but should not be used as a guide to writing or spelling the language.

USE OF DIACRITICS

Diacritics are symbols that may occur with certain letters in a language to aid in its pronunciation. In the Standard presentation of the Mohawk language only the diacritic marking falling tone will occur: à, è, ì, ò, èn. òn. Use of this diacritic signals a long vowel with a slight falling sound (or tone). In Mohawk the occurance of a falling tone signals the appearance of an /h/ or a glottal /'/ in situations when that particular vowel is not being stressed.

okàra   [o-<u>kà:-r</u>a'] *eye*
will occur as:
   skakahraksen   [ska-<u>kah-rá</u>k-sen'] *poor eyes (pickerel)*

ohswènkara   [o<u>hs-wèn:</u>-ka-ra'] *board*
will occur as:
   ohswen'karàke   [o<u>hs-wen'</u>-ka-<u>r</u>à:-ke'] *on the board*

ACCENT

All words in Mohawk have only one accent. In the pronunciation guide given for each word the accented syllable will be marked with a rising or falling tone marker: tá, tà. The accent markers indicate where the word is to recieve the most stress in pronunciation. In most cases the accent is normally on the second to last syllable unless the final syllable ends with vowel *e*. The accent any word receives is set and may not shift about during active speech. The exception occurs when the word acquires a prefix, suffix, , prefix-suffix combination, or situations of incorporation. Then the accent will occur according to shape of the new word.

kahyatonhsera   [ka-hya-tónh-se-ra']   book

kahyatonhseràke   [ka-hya-tonh-se-rà:-keh] on the book

STRESS

The accented syllable of all words in Mohawk may recieve either a short stress or a long stress when pronounced. Short stress indicates a quick pronunciation of the accented syllable, whereas long stress indicates a drawn out pronunciation of the accented syllable. In the pronunciation guide given for each word in this booklet long stress is indicated by a collon accompanying the accented syllable:

Short Stress	*ohonte*	[ó-hon-te']	grass
Long Stress	*okara*	[o-ká:-ra']	*story*
	okàra	[o-kà:-ra']	*eye(s)*

ENGLISH GLOSSES

All translations and interpretations of expressions, often referred to as 'glosses', are provided in italics. It should be noted that these glosses in most cases provide a general meaning or interpretation. The Mohawk language should be learned as it exists and not as a mirror image of English.

INTRODUCTION DIALOGUE

The following dialogue provides some phrases, questions and statements useful in introducing oneself to another.

Mike - *Sekoh, skennen ken.*
     [Sé:-koh, skén-nen' kén]
     Hello, Are you well?

Bill - *Hen'en, skennen'kowa. Nok n'ise.*
     [Hén:'-enh, sken-nen'-kó:-wah. Nok ní:-se']
     Yes, quite well. And yourself

Mike - *Yoyaneratye' n'iih.*
     [Yo-ya-ne-rá-tye' ní:'-ih]
     Things are going good for me.

Bill - *Oh nahòten yesayats.*
     [Oh na-hò:-ten' ye-sá:-yats]
     What's your name?

Mike - *Wihshe yonkyats. Oh nahòten n'ise yesayats.*
     [Wîhs-he yón:-kyats. Oh na-hò:-ten' ní:-se' ye-sá:-yats]
     I'm Mike (they call me Mike). What do they call you?

Bill - **Waryan n'ïïh yonkyats.**
       [War-yá:n ní:'-ih yón:-kyats]
       They call me Bill.

Mike - **Ka' nonwe nitisenon.**
       [Ka' nón:-we' ni-ti-sé:-non']
       Where are you from?

Bill - **Toronto nitiwakenon.**
       [To-rón:-toh ni-ti-wa-ké:-non']
       I'm from Toronto.

Mike - **Onhka nen' ne'e.**
       [ónh-ka nen' né:'-eh]
       Who is that?

Bill - **Sose nen' ne'e. Yonkyatenron.**
       [Só:-seh nen' né:'-eh. Yon-kya-tén:-ron']
       That's Joe. He's my friend.

Mike - **Onen ki' wahi.**
       [O:-nen' ki' wá-hi']
       Good-bye for now

Bill - **Yoh.**
       [Yóh]
       So-long.

* * * * * * * *

On the following pages you will find additional vocabulary, expressions, questions, answers, and descriptions that can be easily incorporated into the sample dialogue given above.

TSI TETSYATATERA'S
When Greeting Each Other

Sekoh [Sé:-koh]
> *Hello!*

Sekoh orye [Se-koh ór-ye' / Se-koh ó-ri' / Se-kó-ri']
> *Hello friend!*

Sekoh kyase' [Se-koh kyá:-se']
> *Hello cousin!*

Sekoh Ihsta'ah [Se-koh Ihs-tá:'-ah / Se-kihs-tá:]
> *Hello Auntie!*

Sekoh rakenoha'ah [Se-koh ra-ke-no-há:'-ah]
> *Hello Uncle!*

Some speakers from different territories or different parts of the same territory may use greetings like the ones shown below.

Skennen'kowa [Sken-nen'-kó:-wah]
> *Great Peace!*

Khwe khwe [Khweh khwéh]
> *Hello hello!*

NAHO'TENHSON AHSHERI'WANONTONHSE
Questions to Ask

Skennen ken. [Skén:-nen' kén]
Are you well (emotionally)?

Hen'en, akwekon skennen. [Hén:'-enh, a-kwé:-kon skén:-nen']
All's well. / everything's fine.

Oh niyohtonhatye'. [Oh ni-yoh-ton-há-tye']
How's it going? / How are things doing?

Yoyaneratye'. [Yo-ya-ne-rá-tye']
It's going well / Things are doing well.

Sata'karite ken. [Sa-ta'-ka-rí:-te' kén]
Are you well (physically)?

Wakata'karite. [Wa-ka-ta'-ka-rí:-te']
I'm well (physically).

Ka' nonwe' nisayo'te'. [Ka- nón:-we' ni-sa-yó'-te']
Where are you working?

Oh nahòten' nonwa sayó'te'. [Oh na-hò:-ten' sa-yó'-te']
What are you presently working at?

ONKWEHOKON
People

owira [o-wí:-ra']
>   baby

raksa'ah [rak-sá:'-ah]
>   boy

yeksa'ah [yek-sá:'-ah]
>   girl

onkwe [ón:-kwe']
>   person

ronkwe [rón:-kwe']
>   man

yakonkwe [ya-kón:-kwe']
>   woman

rokstenha [roks-tén-ha' / roks-tén:'-ah]
>   old man

akokstenha [a-koks-tén-ha' / a-koks-tén:'-ah]
>   old woman

ranekenhteron [ra-ne-kénh-te-ron']
>   young man

tsyakothonwisen [tsya-kot-hon-wí:-sen']
>   young woman

ONHKA NEN' NE'E
Who is it?

Onhka nen ne'e. [ónh-ka' nen' né:'-eh]
Who is it / that?

Onhka nen' ne'e thiken'. [ónh-ka' nen' né:-'eh thí:-ken']
Who is that one?

Onhka thiken'. [ónh-ka' thí:-ken']
Who is that (one)?

Sose nen' ne'e. [Só:-seh nen' né:-'eh]
It's Joe.

Sose nen' ne'e thiken'. [Só:-seh nen' né:-'eh thí:-ken']
That one is Joe.

Etsyenteri' ken. [Ets-yen-té:-ri' kén]
Do you know him?

Hen'en, Riyenteri [Hén:-'enh Ri-yen-té:-ri']
Yes, I know him

Sheyenteri ken. [She-yen-té:-ri' kén]
Do you know her?

Hen'en, kheyenteri [Hén:-'enh, khe-yen-té:-ri']
Yes, I know her.

OH NAHOTEN YESAYATS
What's Your Name?

Oh nahòten yesayats. [Oh na-hò:-ten' ye-sá:-yats]
What is your name / what do they call you?

Tawit yonkyats. [Tá:-wit yón-kyats]
My name is Mike.

Oh nahòten' ronwayats. [Oh na-hò:-ten' ron-wá:-yats]
What is his name / what do they call him?

Wihshe ronwayats. [Wíhshe' ron-wá:-yats]
His name is Mike.

Oh nahòten' yontatyats. [Oh na-hò:-ten' yon-tá-tyats]
What is her name / what do they call her?

Wari yontatyats. [Wá:-ri' yon-tá-tyats]
Her name is Mary.

Oh nahòten' konwayats. [Oh na-hò:-ten' kon-wá:-yats]
What is its name / what do they call it?

Rohwhas konwayats. [Róh-whas kon-wá:-yats]
Its name is Rufus
> This last example would only be used when
> referring to animals or non-human creatures.

KA' NONWE NITISENON
Where Are You From?

Ka' nonwe nitisenon. [Ka' nón:-we' ni-ti-sé:-non']
Where are you from?

Tsi yohnawate nitiwakenon. [Tsi yoh-ná:-wa-te' ni-ti-wa-ké:-non']
I'm from Belleville.

Ka' nonwe nithawenon. [Ka' nón:-we' nit-ha-wé:-non']
Where is he from?

Toronto nithawenon. [To-rón:-toh ni-tha-wé:-non']
He's from Toronto.

Ka' nonwe nityakawenon. [Ka' nón:-we' ni-tya-ka-wé:-non']
Where is she from?

Ohsweken nityakawenon'. [Ohs-we':-ken' ni-tya-ka-wé:-non']
She's from Ohsweken.

Ka' nonwe nityawenon. [Ka' nón:-we' ni-tya-wé:-non']
Where is it from?

Othorèke nityawenon'. [O-tho-rè:-keh ni-tya-wé:-non']
It's from the North.

TSI NAHO'TENHSON NIYONTATIS
Expressions One Uses

Hen'en. [hén:'-enh]
  Yes!

Yah. [yáh]
  No!

Yahten'. [yáh-ten']
  It is not!

Wahi. [wá-hi']
  Isn't it?

Hao' ki' wahi. [há-o' ki' wá-hi']
  Alright / Okay!

khere' ki' wahi. [khé:-re' ki' wá-hi']
  I suppose so.

Tòkah. [tò:-kah]
  I don't know.

Toka' nonwa. [to-ka' nón:-wa']
  Maybe.

Ki' onhte wahi. [ki' onh-te' wá-hi']
  Probably / Possibly.

Tohske' wahi. [tohs-ke' wá-hi']
  It is so.

TSI NISERI'WANONTONS
Things You Ask About.

Oh nahòten. [Oh na-hò:-ten']
    What (is it)?

Oh ne' nahòten. [Oh ne' na-hò:-ten']
    What is that?

Ka' nonwe. [Ka' nón:-we']
    Where (is it)?

Ka' nonkati. [Ka' non-ká:-ti']
    Which way (is it)?

Ka' nikayen'. [Ka' ni-ká:-yen']
    Which one?

Onhka. [ónh-ka']
    Who?

Onhka thiken'. [ónh-ka' thí:-ken']
    Who is that?

Katke. [Kát-keh]
    When?

Oh niyotyeren. [Oh ni-yo-tyé:-ren']
    Why?

Oh nahòten karihonni. [Oh na-hò:-ten' ka-ri-hón:-ni']
    Why / What's the reason?

Oh niyoht. [Oh ní:-yoht]
    How (is it)?

To niyore. [To ni-yó:-re']
    How far (is it)?

To niyotkate. [To ni-yot-ká:-te']
    How often (is it)?

To nikon. [To ní:-kon']
    How many (are there)? (inanimate things)

To nikonti. [To ni-kón:-ti']
    How many of them (are there)? (animate things)

To niyenhs [To ní:-yenhs]
    How long is it?

To niwat. [To ní:-wat]
    How big is it?

To niyokste. [To ni-yóks-te']
    How heavy is it? (inanimate things)

To niyeya'takste [To ni-ye-ya'-táks-te']
    How heavy is it? (animate things)

Onen ken. [o-nen' kén]
    Is it ready?

SHEHRORI TSI NAYONTYERE'
Commands

Kats. [ká:ts]
> Come here!

Wahs. [Wáhs]
> Go away!

Anyon' oksa. [há-nyon' ók-sa']
> Hurry up / hurry along

To takhrori. [to tak-hró:-ri]
> Tell me!

To takyenawa's. [to ta-kyé:-na-wa's]
> Help me!

To takena'tonhahs. [to ta-ke-na'-tón-hahs]
> Show me!

Ka-takon. [ka-tá:-kon]
> Give it to me!

To-taktsiron [to-tak-tsí:-ron]
> Give me a light!

To-takhnekiron [to-tak-hne-kí:-ron]
> Give me a drink / some water!

Totek. [tó:-tek]
> Be quiet!

Satahonhsatat. [sa-ta-hónh-sa-tat]
    Listen!

Se'nikònrarak. [se'-ni-kòn:-ra-rak]
    Be careful!

Tehsta'n. [téhs-ta'n]
    Stand up / Stop (moving)!

Satkahw [sát-kahf]
    Quit (doing something)!

Satyen. [sá-tyen]
    Sit down!

Ka-satqweya't. [kah-sa-tá-we-ya't]
    Come in!

Kenh nonwe tahsahw [kenh non-ká: táh-sahf]
    Bring it over here!

Satatyenawa's. [sa-ta-tyé:-na-wa's]
    Help yourself!

Tohsa. [tóh-sa']
    Don't.

Tohsa ahsatsterihst. [tóh-sa' ah-sats-té:-rihst]
    Don't touch it!

Tohsa natsyer. [tóh-sa' ná-tsyer]
    Don't do that!

OH NIYOHT N'ISE
How Are You?

Wakatshennonni. [wa-kats-hen-nón:-ni']
   I am happy.

Wake'nikonhraksen. [wa-ke'-ni-konh-rák-sen']
   I'm sad.

Wakatonnhahere. [wa-ka-tonn-há-he-re']
   I'm glad.

Wakeserenhtara's. [wa-ke-se-rénh-ta-ra's]
   I'm sleepy.

Tewakhwihshenheyon. [te-wak-hwihs-hen-hé:-yon']
   I'm tired.

Wakenonhwaktani. [wa-ke-nonh-wák-ta-ni']
   I'm sick.

Katonhkarya'ks. [ka-tonh-kár-ya'ks]
   I'm hungry.

Wakenya'tathenhs. [wa-ke-nya'-tát-henhs]
   I'm thirsty.

Kewihstos. [ke-wíhs-tos]
   I'm cold.

Waka'tarihen'. [wa-ka'-ta-rí-hen']
   I'm hot.

TO NIKON
How Many?

Eso nikon. [E-soh ní:-kon']
>> There are a lot (of them).

Sotsi eso. [So-tsih é:-soh]
>> There are too many.

Sotsi ne' eso. [so-tsih ne' é:-soh]
>> That's too many.

eso [é:-soh]
>> many

yawe'towanen' [ya-we'-to-wá:-nen']
>> a lot

Tahsàrat. [Tah-sà:-rat]
>> Count!

Oyeri niyore tahsàrat [O-yé:-rih ni-yó:-reh tah-sà:-rat]
>> Count to ten.

enhska [énhs-ka']
>> one

tekeni [té-ke-ni']
>> two

ahsen [áh-sen']
>> three

kayeri [ka-yé:-ri']
   four

wisk [wísk]
   five

yayak [yá:-ya'k]
   six

tsyata [tsyà:-ta']
   seven

sha'tekon [sha'-té:-kon']
   eight

tyohton [tyóh-ton']
   nine

oyeri [o-yé:-ri']
   ten

To nikon' sayen'. [To ní:-kon' sá:-yen']
   How many do you have?

Ahsen niwakyen'. [áh-sen' ni-wák-yen']
   I have three.

Eso niwakyen'. [é:-so ni-wák-yen']
   I have a lot (of them).

OH NIWAHSOHKOTEN
What Colour Is It?

Oh niwenhseròten'. [oh ni-wenh-se-rò:-ten']
What colour is it (naturally)?

Oh niwahsohkò:ten'. [oh ni-wah-soh-kò:-ten']
What colour is it (dyed, artificially coloured)?

Onekwenhtara niwahsohkòten [o-ne-kwénh-ta-ra' ní:-wah-soh-kò:-ten'
It is red.

Orònya [o-ròn:-ya']
blue

Ohonte [ó-hon-te']
green

Otsinekwar [o-tsí-ne-kwar]
yellow

Athehsa [a-théh-sa']
brown

Ata'kènra [a-ta'-kèn:-ra']
grey

Kahontsi' [ka-hón:-tsi']
black

Kenraken' [ken-rá:-ken']
white

OH NIWENHNISEROTEN
What Kind Of Day Is IT?

Wehniseriyo. [Weh-ni-se-rí:-yo']
It's a nice day.

Niwehniseriyo na'a. [Ni-weh-ni-se-rí:-yo' ná:'-ah]
It is such a nice day!

Yo'tarihen. [Yo'-ta-rí-hen']
It's hot.

Yothore. [Yot-hó:-re']
It's cold.

Yaote. [Ya-ó-te']
It's windy.

Yowerano. [Yo-wé:-ra-no']
It's a cold wind.

Yokennoren. [Yo-ken-nó:-ren']
It's raining.

Yo'keren'enh. [Yo'-ke-rén:'-enh]
It's snowing.

Yoronhyòron. [Yo-ronh-yò:-ren']
It's cloudy.

Yoweren. [Yo-wé:-ren']
It's thundering.

OWENNAHSON'A

The following is an alphabetical (English) listing of the vocabulary that has appeared in this book.

alright *Hao' ki' wahi.* [há-o' ki' wá-hi'] Alright / Okay!

baby *owira* [o-wí:-ra']

barrel *ka'nahkwa* [ka'-náh-kwa']

black *Kahontsi'.* [ka-hón:-tsi'] It is black.

blue *Orònya* [o-ròn:-ya'] blue.

board *ohswènkara* [ohs-wèn:-ka-ra']

book *kahyatonhsera* [ka-hya-tónh-se-ra']

boy *raksa'a* [rak-sá:'-ah]

bring *Kenh nonwe tahsahw* [kenh nón:-we táh-sahf] Bring it over here!

brown *Athehsa* [a-théh-sa']

buy *aetewahninon'* [a-e-te-wah-ní:-non'] You & I should buy it.

car *kàsere'* [kà:-se-re']

careful *Se'nikònrarak.* [se'-ni-kòn:-ra-rak] Be careful!

clay *o'tàra* [o'-tà:-ra']

cloudy *Yoronhyòron.* [Yo-ronh-yò:-ren'] It's cloudy.

cold wind *Yowerano.* [Yo-wé:-ra-no'] It's a cold wind.

cold *Yothore.* [Yot-hó:-re'] It's cold.

cold *Kewihstos.* [ke-wíhs-tos] I'm cold.

come *Kats.* [ká:ts] Come here!

come in *Ka-sataweya't.* [kah-sa-tá-we-ya't] Come in!

coming *tàre'* [tà:-re'] He is coming.

count *Tahsàrat* [Tah-sà:-rat] Count!

don't *Tohsa.* [tóh-sa'] Don't. *Tohsa ahsatsterihst.* [tóh-sa' ah-sats-té:-rihst] Don't touch it!

ear *ohonhsa* [o-hónh-sa'] (inner) ear

enter *kataweyàtha'* [ka-ta-we-yà:-t-ha'] I enter a place.

eye *okàra* [o-kà:-ra']

finger *ohsnonhsa* [oh-snónh-sa']

flower *otsitsya* [o-tsì:-tsya']

girl *yeksa'a* [yek-sá:'-ah]

give *Ka-takon.* [ka-tá:-kon] Give it
to me! *To-taktsiron* [to-tak-tsí:-ron]
Give me a light! *To-takhnekiron* [to-
tak-hne-kí:-ron] Give me a drink /
some water!

glad *Wakatonnhahere'*.
[wa-ka-tonn-há-he-re'] I'm glad.

go *Wahs*. [Wáhs] Go away!
Aonsakahtenti' [a-on-sa-kah-tén:-ti']
I should go home. *To i tyahtenti* [to i
tyah-tén:-ti] Let's you & I go home.

going *wàke'* [wà:-ke'] I am going.
Yoyaneratye'. [Yo-ya-ne-rá-tye']
It's going well / Things are doing
well. *Oh niyohtonhatye'*. [Oh ni-
yoh-ton-há-tye'] How's it going? /
How are things doing?

grass *ohonte* [ó-hon-te']

green *Ohonte* [ó-hon-te']

grey *Ata'kènra* [a-ta'-kèn:-ra']

hand *ohsnonhsa* [oh-snónh-sa']

happy *Wakatshennonni'*.
[wa-kats-hen-nón:-ni'] I am happy.

Hello *Sekoh* [Sé:-koh] Hello Auntie
Sekoh Ihsta'ah [Se-koh Ihs-tá:'-
ah] Hello friend *Sekoh orye*
[Se-koh ór-ye' / Se-kó-ri'] Hello
Uncle *Sekoh rakenoha'ah*
[Se-koh ra-ke-no-há:'ah]

help *To takyenawa's*. [to ta-
kyé:-na-wa's] Help me!
Satatyenawa's. [sa-ta-tyé:-na-
wa's] Help yourself!

hold *Waka'tarihen*.
[wa-ka'-ta-rí-hen] I'm hot.

hot *Yo'tarihen*. [Yo'-ta-rí-hen']
It's hot.

how *Oh niyoht*. [Oh ní:-yoht]
How (is it)? *To niyore'*. [To ni-
yó:-re'] How far? *To niyotkate'*.
[To ni-yot-ká:-te'] How often?
To nikonti'. [To ni-kón:-ti'] How
many of them (animate things)?
To nikon'. [To ní:-kon'] How
many (inanimate things)?

hungry *Katonhkarya'ks*.
[ka-tonh-kár-ya'ks] I'm hungry.

hurry *Anyon' oksa*. [há-nyon'
ók-sa'] Hurry up / hurry along

know *Etsyenteri' ken*. [Ets-yen-
té:-ri' kén] Do you know him?
Sheyenteri' ken. [She-yen-té:-ri'
kén] Do you know her?

listen *Satahonhsatat.*
[sa-ta-hónh-sa-tat] Listen!

little *nikonha* [ni-kón-ha' /
ni-kón:'-ah] A little (amount of).

lot *yawe'towanen'*
[ya-we'-to-wá:-nen']

man *ronkwe* [rón:-kwe']

many *eso* [é:-soh]

maybe *Toka' nonwa.*
[to-ka' nón:-wa']

money *ohwihsta* [oh-wíhs-ta']

nice day *Wehniseriyo'.*
[Weh-ni-se-rí:-yo'] It's a nice day.

no *Yah.* [yáh]

now *onen* [ó:-nen']

old *akokstenha* [a-koks-tén-ha' /
a-koks-tén:'-ah] old woman;
rokstenha [roks-tén-ha' / roks-tén:'-
ah] old man

pair *oyana* [o-yá:-na']

person *onkwe* [ón:-kwe']

pickerel *skakahraksen*
[ska-kah-rák-sen']

probably *Ki' onhte wahi.*

[ki' onh-te' wá-hi']

quiet *Totek.* [tó:-tek] Be quiet!

quit *Satkahw* [sát-kahf] Quit
(doing something)!

raining *Yokennoren.*
[Yo-ken-nó:-ren'] It's raining.

ready *Onen ken.* [o-nen' kén]
Is it ready? / Okay?

red *Onekwenhtara niwahsohkòten*
[o-ne-kwénh-ta-ra' ni-wah-soh-
kò:-ten'] It is red.

sad *Wake'nikonhraksen'.* [wa-
ke'-ni-konh-rák-sen'] I'm sad.

shoe *ahta* [áh-ta']

show me *To takena'tonhahs.* [to
ta-ke-na'-tón-hahs] Show me!

sick *Wakenonhwaktani'.* [wa-ke-
nonh-wák-ta-ni'] I'm sick.

sit *Satyen.* [sá-tyen] Sit down!

sleepy *Wakeserenhtara's.* [wa-ke-
se-rénh-ta-ra's] I'm sleepy.

snowing *Yo'keren'enh.*
[Yo'-ke-rén:'-enh] It's snowing.

speaking *wakthare'* [wák-tha-re']
I am speaking.

stand up *Tehsta'n.* [téhs-ta'n]
Stand up / Stop (moving)!

story *okara* [o-ká:-ra']

suppose so *khere' ki' wahi.*
[khé:-re' ki' wá-hi'] I suppose so.

tell *Shehrori* [s-heh-ró:-ri] Tell her /
them! *Takwahrori* [ta-kwah-ró:-ri']
Tell me!

thirsty *Wakenya'tathenhs.*
[wa-ke-nya'-tát-henhs] I'm thirsty.

thundering *Yoweren.* [Yo-wé:-ren']
It's thundering.

tired *Tewakhwihshenheyon.*
[te-wak-hwihs-hen-hé:-yon']
I'm tired.

told *wa'khehrori'* [wa'-kheh-ró:-ri']
I told her / them.

too many *Sotsi eso.* [So-tsih é:-soh]
There are too many. *Sotsi ne' eso.*
[so-tsih ne' é:-soh] That's too
many.

turtle *a'nowara* [a'-nó:-wa-ra']

use *katstha'* [káts-tha'] I use.

waist *ohsyàkara* [oh-syà:-ka-ra']

well *Skennen ken.* [Skén:-nen' kén]
Are you well (emotionally)?

Hen'en,, akwekon skennen.
Hén:'-en, a-kwé:-kon skén:-nen']
All's well. / everything's fine.
Sata'karite ken. [Sa-ta'-ka-rí:-te'
kén] Are you well (physically)?
Wakata'karite. [Wa-ka-ta'-ka-rí:-
te'] I'm well (physically).

what *Oh nahòten.* [Oh na-hò:-
ten'] What (is it)? *Oh ne'
nahòten.* [Oh ne' na-hò:-ten']
What's that? *Oh nisatyerha'* [Oh
nih-sa-tyér-ha'] What are you
doing? *Oh niwenhseròten'.* [oh
ni-wenh-se-rò:-ten'] What colour
(naturally)? *Oh niwahsohkò:ten'.*
[oh ni-wah-soh-kò:-ten'] What
colour is it (dyed, coloured)?

when *Katke.* [Kát-keh] *When?*

where *Ka' nonwe.* [Ka' nón:-we']
Where (is it)? *Ka' wahse'.* [Ka'
wáh-se'] Where are you going?

which *Ka' nonkati.* [Ka' non-ká:-
ti'] Which way? *Ka' nikayen'.*
[Ka' ni-ká:-yen'] Which one?

white *Kenraken.* [ken-rá:-ken']
It is white.

who *Onhka nen ne'e.* [ónh-ka'
nen' né:'-eh] Who is it? *Onhka
nen' ne'e thiken'.* Who is that?

why *Oh niyotyeren.*
[Oh ni-yo-tyé:-ren'] Why

windy *Yaote.* [Ya-ó-te'] It's windy.

woman *yakonkwe* [ya-kón:-kwe']

word *owenna* [o-wén-na']

working *Ka' nonwe nisayo'te'.*
[Ka' nón:-we nisa-yó'-te']
Where are you working?

year *ohsera* [óh-se-ra']

yellow **Otsinekwar**
[o-tsí-ne-kwar] yellow

yes **hen'en.** [hén:'-enh]

you **ise** [í:-se']

young **tsyakothonwisen**
[tsya-kot-hon-wí:-sen'] young
woman; **ranekenhteron** [ra-ne-
kénh-te-ron'] young man

Part 2

CONTENTS

* * * * * * * * *

PRONUNCIATION

The Mohawk language, represented by this writing system, uses twelve (12) letters (a, e, h, i, k, n, o, r, s, t, w, y) and a symbol to represent the glottal -'- (also considered to be a consonant). For a more indepth description of pronunciation see Book 1.

Vowel		Pronunciation	English	Notes
a	*ahta*	[áh-ta']	shoe	like *a* in 'f<u>a</u>ther'
e	*wàke'*	[wà:-ke']	I'm going	like *e* in 'th<u>e</u>y'
	kàsere'	[kà:-se-re']	car	like *e* in 'm<u>e</u>t'
i	*ise*	[í:-se']	you	like *ee* in 's<u>ee</u>'
o	*ohsera*	[óh-se-ra']	year	like *o* in 'n<u>o</u>te'
en	*owenna*	[o-wén:-na']	word	like *u* in 's<u>u</u>n'
on	*ohonhsa*	[o-hónh-sa']	ear	like *oo* in 's<u>oo</u>n'

Consonant		Pronunciation	English	Notes
k	*kàsere'*	[kà:-se-re']	car	like *g* in 'g<u>a</u>te'
	wakthare	[wák-tha-re']	I'm speaking	like *k* in 'spea<u>k</u>'
t	*tare'*	[tá:-re']	He' coming	like *d* in '<u>d</u>og'
	katstha'	[káts-tha']	I use	like *t* in '<u>t</u>ake'
n	*onen*	[ó:-nen']	now	like *n* in '<u>n</u>ow'
r	*raksa'a*	[rak-sá:'-ah]	boy	like *r* in '<u>r</u>un'
s	*ohsera*	[óh-se-ra']	year	like *s* in 's<u>u</u>n'
	kàsere'	[kà:-se-re']	car	like *z* in '<u>z</u>oo'
w	*owira*	[o-wí:-ra']	baby	like *w* in '<u>w</u>ind'
y	*oyana*	[o-yá:-na']	pair	like *y* in '<u>y</u>es'

NOUNS

Meaningful units of expression, *words*, which act as descriptions of objects, places, or living beings or creatures are referred to as *nouns*. In Mohawk, as in all other languages, it is possible to have as many nouns available as is necessary to adequately describe anything that anyone might want. The structure of the language allows for the constant creation of new vocabulary within the language itself, unlike English which often creates new words using Latin, Greek, or French vocabulary, or draws in vocabulary from other languages.

Mohawk nouns may exhibit a lot of flexibility, often having several different or related meanings, depending upon usuage at the time, or the dialect in which they occur. One thing to keep in mind is that the Iroquoian culture does not place a lot of emphasis on objects or things. Therefore, quite often in Mohawk, there will be only one word where in English they may be several.

atyàtawi'   *coat, shirt, dress, etc..*
(this word refers to anything that covers the upper part of the body)

There are two main classifications of Mohawk nouns: formal, and functional. Formal nouns constitute the bulk of the cultural vocabulary referring to objects, places, concepts, ideas, etc..., and are most often fairly short in length. Functional nouns are those newer words more recently created to describe the contemporary world outside of the traditional culture: words such as **kawennokwas** *'radio'*; **onotsta'kowa** *'elephant'*. Functional nouns may also appear to be double-sided, acting as either noun or verb, their description dependent upon how they are used in active speech.

ratorats. *he hunts*

riyenteri ne ratorats. *I know the hunter.*

(In the second example **ratorats** acts as a noun, but occurs as a verb in the first.)

FORMAL NOUNS

Formal nouns are typically three or four syllables in length. There may also be, though, nouns which are only two syllables or five syllables in length. One characteristic of formal nouns is that they quite often will have two or more English interpretations of what they describe.

> ie.   *oriwa may be interpretated as: business, matter, deal, word, fault, purpose, way of doing.*

The way in which a formal noun is used in the language will help to better define what the interpretation will be. The section on *Noun Incorporation* in this book will look at this in more depth.

Formal nouns are further divided into two categories depending upon the cultural interpretation of the object, place, or individual being described, or the sound of the noun's first syllable.

CATEGORY I. Formal nouns are those which describe an object or place which is subject to change as a result of human interference, human invention, or because of a change in movement or state of the object. Nearly all vocabulary that deals with possessions, artifacts, tools, or manufactured goods belong in this category. In most cases, formal nouns in Category I in most cases begin with *ka* or *a*, or in a few rare cases with *e* or *en*.

KA-nouns often refer to objects of human inventention.

kanonhsa [ka-nónh-sa']	*house / building / dwelling*
kanakta [ka-nák-ta']	*bed / place (area, space)*
katshe' [káts-he']	*bottle / flask / jar*
kanata [ka-ná:-ta']	*town, village, hamlet, city*
kahonweya [ka-hon-wé:-ya']	*boat, ship, punt, rowboat*
karonta [ka-rón:-ta']	*log, tree*

A-nouns often refer to objects of human manufacture or ownership.

ahta' [áh-ta']	*shoe(s) / footwear*
àthere [à:-the-re']	*basket*
atoken' [a-tó:-ken']	*axe / hatchet*
àshare [à:-sha-re']	*knife / sword*
arhya [ár-hya']	*hook / fishhook*
ahsire [áh-si-re']	*blanket*

E/En-nouns represent what are possibly the oldest nouns in the language. In modern speech these nouns are often preceded by *aw*.

erhar [ér-har]	*dog*
ehsa [éh-sa']	*black ash (tree)*
eryahsa	
or *aweryahsa* [a-wer-yáh-sa']	*heart*

CATERGORY II. The second class of formal nouns are those cultural descriptions of an object or place which remain unchanged or constant in appearance and existence, and are not subject to change, alteration, or movement through outside intervention. Nearly all words describing the environment, natural formations and functions, physical and emotional attributes, body parts, and many animal names are members of this category. Formal nouns in Category II in most cases will begin with *o* and in a few cases with *on*.

ohonte [ó-hon-te']	*grass / herbs / green*
otsitsya [o-tsì:-tsya']	*flower / blossom*
oryènta [or-yèn:-ta']	*manner, habit, way of doing*
oweyenna [o-we-yén:-na']	*ability / control / aptitude*
o'nikònra [o'-ni-kòn:-ra']	*spirit / mind / consciousness*

ohsina [oh-sí:-na']	*leg*
okonhsa [o-kónh-sa']	*face / visage*
owenna [o-wén:-na']	*word / voice / speech / tone*
onhwentsya [onh-wén-tsya']	*earth / land / ground*

FUNCTIONAL NOUNS

In most cases, functional nouns are longer than five syllables. They are much more elaborate in their descriptions of objects, places, and individuals. In some cases a functional noun may also act as a simple sentence when occurring as an isolated word. Functional nouns may be grouped into three categories.

CATEGORY I functional nouns are those words which are often simple or elaborate descriptions of an object. Nouns in this category, in most cases, will begin with either *ye, yon, yo,* or occasionally *ka* or *wa,* and will end with either *a* or *e.* A characteristic of the final syllables of Functional nouns is that they will appear as: *hsera, tshera, hkwa, tha, hstha, tahkwa,* or *hstahkwa.*

> *yekhsokewàtha* [yek-hso-ke-wà:-tha']
> > *tea towel (one uses it to dry dishes)*
> *kahyatonhsera* [ka-hya-tónh-se-ra']
> > *book (it is of a written nature)*
> *yekhsoharehtahkwa* [yek-hso-ha-reh-táh-kwa']
> > *dish cloth (one uses it to wash dishes)*
> *yononhsa'tariha'tahkwa* [yo-nonh-sa'-ta-ri-ha'-táh-kwa']
> > *stove / heater (one uses it to heat the house)*
> *yontorihshentahkwa*
> > *sofa / chesterfield (one uses it to rest upon)*
> *wahkwennyatsherarahkwa*
> > *clothes basket / hamper (one uses it to hold clothes)*
> *yetsi'tsyarahkwa*
> > *flower vase / pot (ones uses it to hold flowers)*

CATEGORY II functional nouns are elaborate descriptions of places or locations. They often begin with *ye, yon,* or *yo* and end in *hstha* or *tha*. In most cases the word *tsi* will preceed the entire functional noun being used.

tsi yekhonnyàtha [tsi yek-hon-nyà:-tha']
        kitchen (the place where one cooks)
tsi yontaterihonnyennìtha
        school (the place where one is taught)
tsi yontenhninonhtha
        store (the place where one sells)

CATEGORY III functional nouns create descriptions that refer to individuals, relatives, occupations, or professions. Nearly all nouns in this category will begin with a pronominal prefix (he, she, they, etc...).

raksa'a [rak-sá:-'a]   *boy (he-child-is)*
yeksa'a [yek-sá:-'a]   *girl (she-child-is)*

ronkwe [rón:-kwe']   *man (he-person-is)*
yakonkwe [ya-kón:-kwe']   *woman (she-person-is)*

rake'niha [ra-ke'-ní-ha']   *my father (he/to me father is)*
raktsi'a [rak-tsí:-'a]   *my older brother*
        (he/to me older brother is)

shakorihonnyennis [sha-ko-ri-hon-nyén:-nis]
        teacher (male) (he teaches them)
shakoyenahs [sha-ko-yé:-nahs] *policeman (he catches them)*
rayenthos [ra-yént-hos]   *farmer (he plants)*
rarihstaherha [ra-rihs-ta-hér-ha']
        steel worker (he puts up steel)
ratorats [ra-tó:-rats]   *hunter (he hunts)*

Since the criteria for functional nouns involves elaborate description, some of them can get quite long and fancy. Below I've written one of the all-time favorites, *"stove polish"*.

yontenonhsa'tariha'tahkwatsherahon'tsihstatsherahstara'the'tahkwa
[yon-te-nonh-sa'-ta-ri-ha'-tah-kwats-he-ra-hon'-tsihs-tats-
he-rahs-ta-ra'-the'-táh-kwa']
(the stuff that makes shiney that one puts on thing that is used to heat the house)

BEING DEFINITE ABOUT THE NOUN

When a speaker wants to be definite about what they are talking about the word *ne* is placed directly before the noun being used. Doing this makes the noun it occurs before definite. Using *ne* in this manner creates a pattern similar to the English use of the word *"the"*. When the *ne* word is absent from the statement the resulting interpretation is similar to the English use of *"a"* or *"an"*.

Without *ne*:
Wakhninonh yekhsoharehtahkwa.
[Wak-hní:-nonh yek-hso-ha-reh-táh-kwa']
I bought a dish cloth.

With *ne*:
Wakhninonh ne yekhsoharehtahkwa.
[Wak-hní:-nonh ne yek-hso-ha-reh-táh-kwa']
I bought the dish cloth.

BE CAREFUL: The thing to remember is that *ne* does not mean *the* but that in the situation shown in the example above it creates an interpretation similar to English *the*.

For practice try going through all of the noun vocabulary that you know so far using the *ne* word before each one.

Placing *ne* before any noun, whether formal or functional will create a *definite* sense about that particular word. There are, hoever, certain limitations. Those limitations have to deal primarily with the verb (phrase) you happening to be using at the time. For example, using Formal - Category I nouns you can say;

Wakhninonh ne kanakta.
[wak-hnĺ:-nonh ne ka-nák-ta']
I bought a bed.

But because of the nature of Formal - Category II nouns you can not use all of them with the verb shown above. You could say;

Wakhninonh ne otsitsya. [Wak-hnĺ:-nonh ne o-tsì-tsya']
I bought the flower.

but you could not say;

NO: **Wakhninonh ne o'nikòn:ra.** [Wak-hnĺ:-nonh ne o-tsì-tsya']
I bought the spirit (mind, consciousness).

It doesn't even make sense in English.

All three categories of functional noun can be used with *ne*.

Wakhninonh ne kahyatonhsera. [Wak-hnĺ:-nonh ne ka-hya-tónh-se-ra']
I bought the book.

Wakhninonh ne yontenhninonhtha.
[Wah-hnĺ:-nonh ne yon-tenh-ni-nónh-tha']
I bought the store.

NOTICE that the *tsi* that would usually occur with **yontenhninonhtha** is dropped the word is being treated like a thing and not a place.

(10)

In the examples given on the previous page using Formal - Category I and Functional - Category I & II nouns, the words being used have all been treated as objects. However, this is not the case with Functional Nouns - Category III. These nouns deal with *individuals* and they must agree with or describe *who* is doing the action. Notice the examples shown below, especially the way that *agreement* works.

Rohninonh ne ronkwe. [Roh-ní:-nonh ne rón:-kwe']
The man bought it.

Yakohninonh ne yakonkwe. [Ya-koh-ní:-nonh ne ya-kón:-kwe']
The woman bought it.

Therefore, if you are talking about a *she* or *he* doing some action or involved in some activity, then the word you use to refer to that person must be the same *gender* (i.e., male, or female). *Number* (of individuals involved) is also important.

Rotihninonh ne rononkwe. [Ro-tih-ní:-nonh ne ro-nón:-kwe']
The men bought it.

Yotihninonh ne kononkwe. [Yo-tih-ní:-nonh ne ko-nón:-kwe']
The women bought it.

AGREEMENT between verbs and nouns in Mohawk IS VERY IMPORTANT

So is the way that the words are arranged. The *normal* way of constructing a sentence like the ones shown above is to put *who is doing* directly after the verb (describing the action or activity). If two individuals are involved, the one spoken to or about occurs first after the verb and the one doing the speaking occurs last. The same pattern occurs if objects are spoken of or about.

LOCATING THE ROOT OF THE NOUN

If you've ever had the opportunity to read any of the linguistic material written about the Mohawk language, then you've probably run across the definitions *Noun Root* and *Noun Incorporation*. If not, then this section may prove to be useful as you continue on with the language. Knowledge of these two definitions may make it easier for you to acquire vocabulary quickly and with more ease. It may also help you understand the vocabulary you run across and will allow you to make up some vocabulary of your own.

As mentioned earlier in this book most nouns begin with *ka, o, a, e, en, ye, yon, yo,* or *wa*. The beginning sounds are called *Nominal Prefixes*. These Nominal Suffixes provide an *"it / one"* introduction to most nouns. The sounds *a* and *e* at the end of most nouns are called the *Nominal Suffixes*. These suffixes create a verbal (*is / are*) aspect to the nouns. Given this, one could easily interpret nouns as simple sentences.

kahyatonhsera
(it) book (is) / (it's a) book.

Earlier in the section on formal nouns I showed you that the nominal prefixes *ka* and *o* were instrumental in defining the two categories. The main reason for this is revealed in the actual meaning or intention of the prefixes. Prefix *ka* gives the notion of movement or action, while prefix *o* creates the notion of static, or non-movement. Prefix *a*, though, provides a sense of reflexiveness (action benefiting someone). This may help to explain its relationship with personal possessions and tools. Prefixes *ye, yon,* and *yo* are pronominals (prefixed pronouns) that normally occur with verbs. They provide a *"one / they"* or *"it is"* aspect to the noun's interpretation.

yononhsa'tariha'tahkwa
(one uses / they use (it) to heat the house)
(it is used to heat the house)

Thus the nominal prefixes and the nominal suffixes have their own meaning. The actual *nominal* part of the noun, (the Noun Root) occurs between the prefix and the suffix. Therefore, if you wish to locate the noun root, you will have to eliminate the prefix and the suffix of the word.

Nominal	minus prefix	minus suffix	NOUN ROOT
kanata town	(ka)*nata*	-*nat*(a)	*-nat-*
onenhste corn	(o)*nenhste*	-*nenhst*(e)	*-nenhst-*
owira baby	(o)*wira*	-*wir*(a)	*-wir-*

Note that nominal prefixes on words that begin with *a* and *e* or *en* are considered to be part of the noun root. These may not be eliminated.

Nominal	minus prefix	minus suffix	NOUN ROOT
àthere basket	Ø	*àther*(e)	*-a'ther-* *
àshare knife	Ø	*àshar*(e)	*-a'shar-* *
eryahsa heart	Ø	*eryahs*(a)	*-eryahs-* **

* When *à* occurs before a *k*, *t*, or *s*, and that particular syllable is not recieving stress, then *à* will occur as *a'*. This is the reason for the two noun roots shown above occurring as *-a'ther-* and *-a'shar-*.

** Many nouns that begin with *e* or *en* will often have *aw* attached as the first sound. Look back at *Formal Nouns Category I*.

In Mohawk dictionaries where nouns are listed by their roots a hyphen, "-", will occur at the beginning and end of the noun.

LOCATING THE VERB BASE

Mohawk verbs consists of two parts: the *Pronominal Prefix*, the element in that describes who or what is taking part in the action or activity; and the *Verb Base*, that part of the verb that describes the action or activity. Below is shown where the division occurs between these two elements.

VERB	Pronominal Prefix	Verb Base
wakhninonh I bought	**wak-** I	**-hninonh** bought / did buy
wakyen´ I have	**wak-** I	**-yen´** have
sahninonh You bought	**sa-** you	**-hninonh** bought / did buy
sayen´ You have	**sa-** you	**-yen´** have
rohninonh He bought	**ro-** he	**-hninonh** bought / did buy
royen´ He has	**ro-** he	**-yen´** have
yakohninonh She bought	**yako** she	**-hninonh** bought / did buy
yakoyen´ She has	**yako** she	**-yen´** have
rotihninonh They bought	**roti-** they (males)	**-hninonh** bought / did buy
rotiyen´ They have	**roti-** they (males)	**-yen´** have
yotihninonh They bought	**yoti** they (females)	**-hninonh** bought / did buy
yotiyen´ They have	**yoti** they (females)	**-yen´** have

Pronouns for the 3rd person plural *they*, may indicate male or female individuals. Male *they* pronominal refers to either males only or a group of males and females, but female *they* pronominal refers to females only.

NOUN INCORPORATION

Now comes the fun part. Since you have spent some time looking learning to recognize the pronominal prefixes and the verb bases you should now be ready to tackle something like *Noun Incorporation*. This term refers to the productive Mohawk process used to create expressions, phrases and whole sentences that will appear as complete words. The process is quite simple. You make use of the noun roots, such as those you already seen in this book, and you then place them inside verbs, between the pronominals and the verb bases.

First of all, let's look at why nouns are incorporated into verbs. First you looked at how nouns are treated as definite things in relation to the verb. You did that by placing *ne* before the noun. But if you want to make a very general statement about the noun, then you will incorporate the noun right into the verb you are using. Let's look at the examples given below.

Wakhninonh ne onenhste. [Wak-hní:-nonh ne ó:-nenhs-teh]
I bought the corn.
That is, I bought a particular amount of corn, or possible all the corn that was available.

Wakhninonh onenhste. [Wak-hní:-nonh ó:-nenhs-teh]
I bought a corn.
That is, the was corn available, but I bought only one piece.

Wakenenhstahninonh. [Wa-ke-nenhs-tah-ní:-nonh]
I bought corn.
That is, of all of the things that I do as a rule, buying corn is one of them.
Therefore I could say that "I am a corn buyer."

Incorporated-noun verb phrases are used extensively in Mohawk. This makes it possible to create lots of expressions and statements.

Anything that you would do as a habit or as a general course of action can be expressed through noun incorporation. There are, however, limitations. Nouns describing specific individuals, locations, relations, or animal names CAN NOT BE INCORPORATED. Most other can be.

As I've already stated, incorporating nouns can be quite simple. There are, however, a few things to keep in mind. If the verb base begins with a consonant (ie. *-hninonh bought*) you will have to place a connector (vowel or syllable combination) between the incorporated noun (root) and the verb base. The same is true for pronominal prefixes. With most nouns this connector will be *a*, except in cases where the noun ends with a *glottal ʼ* such as *atyàtawiʼ*. In this case the connector may occur as *tshera* or *hkwa*. The trickiest pronominal prefixes is *wak*. It will change to *wake* when used before noun roots beginning with a consonant. *Ro* and *yako* before noun roots beginning with *a* will still occur as *ro* and *yako*. The *a* of the *a*-noun root is deleted, but only in these two cases. The following two examples show the process you use to incorporate a noun beginning with a consonant and with *a*.

Pronominal	Noun Root	Connector	Verb Base
wake	*-nenhst-*	*-a-*	*-hninonh*

wakenenhstahninonh [wa-ke-nenhs-tah-níː-nonh]
I bought corn / I was a corn buyer.

sa	*-nenhst-*	*-a-*	*-hninonh*

sanenhstahninonh [sa-nenhs-tah-níː-nonh]
You bought corn / You were a corn buyer.

ro	*-nenhst-*	*-a-*	*-hninonh*

ronenhstahninonh [ro-nenhs-tah-níː-nonh]
He bought corn / he was a corn buyer.

Pronominal	Noun Root	Connector	Verb Base
yako	*-nenhst-*	*-a-*	*-hninonh*

yakonenhstahninonh [ya-ko-nenhs-tah-ní:-nonh]
She bought corn / She was a corn buyer.

roti	*-nenhst-*	*-a-*	*-hninonh*

rotinenhstahninonh [ro-ti-nenhs-tah-ní:-nonh]
They bought corn / They were corn buyers.

yoti	*-nenhst-*	*-a-*	*-hninonh*

yotinenhstahninonh [yo-ti-nenhs-tah-ní:-nonh]
They bought corn / They were corn buyers.

Pronominal	Noun Root	Connector	Verb Base
wak	*-atya'tawi'-*	*-tshera-*	*-hninonh*

wakatya'atawi'tsherahninonh [wa-ka-tya'-ta-wi'ts-he-rah-ní:-nonh]
I bought a coat / I was a coat buyer.

sa	*-atya'tawi'-*	*-tshera-*	*-hninonh*

satya'tawi'tsherahninonh [sa-tya'ta-wi'ts-he-rah-ní:-nonh]
You bought a coat / You were a coat buyer.

ro	*-atya'tawi'-*	*-tshera-*	*-hninonh*

rotya'atawi'tsherahninonh [ro-tya'-ta-wi'ts-he-rah-ní:-nonh]
He bought a coat / He was a coat buyer.

yako	*-atya'tawi'-*	*-tshera-*	*-hninonh*

yakotya'tawi'tsherahninonh [ya-ko-tya'ta-wi'ts-he-rah-ní:-nonh]
She bought a coat / She were a coat buyer.

Pronominal	Noun Root	Connector	Verb Base
ron	-atya'tawi'-	-tshera-	-hninonh

ronatya'atawi'tsherahninonh [ro-na-ka-tya'-ta-wi'ts-he-rah-nî:-nonh]
They bought coats / They were coat buyers.

yon	-atya'tawi'-	-tshera-	-hninonh

yonatya'tawi'tsherahninonh [yo-na-tya'ta-wi'ts-he-rah-nî:-nonh]
They bought coats / They were coat buyers.

In the set of examples showing the incorporation of a noun beginning with *a* you will have noticed that the *they* pronominal prefixes occur as **yon** and **ron**. This will always occur with incorporated-noun verb phrases where the noun begins with *a*, otherwise, the pronominals you use will look like the ones shown with the *-nenhst-* example.

With the pronominals provided so far, try now to create additional verb phrases on your own. Use the examples given below as a starting base. Use all of the pronominals that you have seen used in the previous sections. Write the verb phrases out in sets similar to the way they have been presented here.

wakhwihstayen' [wak-hwîhs-ta-yen'] *I have money.*

wakatya'tawi'tsherayen' [wa-ka-tya'-ta-wi'ts-he-rá:-yen'] *I have a coat.*

wakenenhstayen' [wa-ke-nénhs-ta-yen'] *I have corn.*

wakhyatonhserayen' [wak-hya-tonh-se-rá:-yen'] *I have a book.*

wakahtahkwayen' [wa-kah-táh-kwa-yen'] *I have shoes.*

wakahsirayen' [wa-kah-si-rá:-yen'] *I have a blanket.*

wakenonhsayen' [wa-ke-nónh-sa-yen'] *I have a house.*

THIS OR THAT? - USING DEMONSTRATIVES

In the discussion on making a noun definite I introduced you to the word *ne*. Now I will show how you may be specific about the noun you're using. To do this requires that you make use of two phrases: *tho' iken' there it is* and *kenh iken' here it is*. In fact they are short sentences, but when they are used before a noun quite often they are shortened to *thiken'* and *kiken'*. The technical term for this is *Demonstrative*. These words are used to create *that* and *this* phrases. Look at the pattern shown below and then practice it same with any of the other nouns you have learned.

thiken' kahyatonhsera [thí:-ken' ka-hya-tónh-se-ra'] *that book*

kiken' kahyatonhsera [kí:-ken' ka-hya-tónh-se-ra'] *this book*

thiken raksa'a [thí:-ken' rak-sá:-'ah] *that boy*

kiken' raksa'a [kí:-ken' rak-sá:-'ah] *this boy*

thiken' erhar [thí:-ken' ér-har] *that dog*

kiken' erhar [kí:-ken' ér-har] *this dog*

It is now possible to make short sentences out of the phrases shown above. All you do is place word *ne'e* between the demonstrative and the noun. This creates a *this is / that is a...* type of sentence.

Thiken' ne'e kahyatonhsera.
[Thí:-ken' né:'eh ka-hya-tónh-se-ra'] *That is a book*

Kiken' ne'e raksa'a [Kí:-ken' né:'eh rak-sá:-'ah] *This is a boy*

Thiken' ne'e erhar [Thí:-ken' né:'eh ér-har] *That is a dog*

Kiken' ne'e àshare [Kí:-ken' né:'eh a':-sha-re'] *This is a knife.*

Using the phrase *Kiken' ne'e* and *Kiken' ne'e* create a type of declarative statement, that is, you indicate what something or someone is. The word order can be turned around if you want to emphasize the noun rather than the demonstrative one. The noun you are emphasizing would then be placed directly in front of the statement.

> *Kahyatonhsera ne'e kiken'.* [Ka-hya-tónh-se-ra' né:-'eh kí:-ken']
> *This is a BOOK.*

> *Erhar ne'e thiken'.* [Ér-har né:-'eh thí:-ken'] *That is a DOG.*

Try creating more sentences like this with the vocabulary you have learned. If you wanted to make a question where the answer might be one of the statements shown above, you would use the question word *ken*. You must place this word directly after the noun.

Kahyatonhsera ken ne'e kiken'. [Ka-hya-tónh-se-ra' kén né:-'eh kí:-ken']
> *Is this a BOOK.*

Kahyatonhsera ken ne'e thiken'. [Ka-hya-tónh-se-ra' kén né:-'eh thí:-ken']
> *Is that a BOOK.*

Another question that you could use asks *what something is (specifically)*. The answer you give would look exactly like the samples shown at the top of this page.

> *Oh nahòten ne'e kiken'* [Oh na-hò:-ten' né:-'eh kí:-ken']
> *What is this (thing)?*

> *Oh nahòten ne'e thiken'* [Oh na-hò:-ten' né:-'eh thí:-ken']
> *What is that (thing)?*

Practice using both question types with Mohawk speakers to elicit more vocabulary on you own. This way you will discover the names of things and objects without having to attach an English name to them.

LOCATING A PLACE

Creating a location in Mohawk can be easily done by attaching a suffix to the noun. This particular set of suffixes are often referred to as Locatives. Attaching these suffixes requires the removal of the nominal suffix *a*, and with some nouns the use of connectors *atsher-*, *ahser-*, or *ahkw-*. Below are provided the four most commonly used Locatives.

-àke is a locative that interprets as *on*. In some cases it may also be interpreted as *in*, *to* or *at*.

    kanonhsa house
        kanonhsàke [ka-nonh-sà:-keh] on the house
    onhwentsya ground
        onhwentsyàke [on-hwen-tsyà:-keh] on the ground
    kahyatonhsera book
        kahyatonhseràke [ka-hya-tonh-se-rà:-keh] on the book
    ahta' shoe(s)
        ahtahkwàke [ah-tah-kwà:-keh] on the shoe(s)
    atyàtawi" coat, shirt, dress
        atya'tawi'tsheràke [a-tya'-ta-wi'ts-he-rà:-keh] on the coat...
    kerhite tree
        kerhitàke [ker-hi-tà:-keh] on / in the tree

There are a few nouns which will require the suffix *-hne* instead of *-àke*. Nouns which take *hne* will have to be learned as they occur.

    atehkwàra table
        atehkwahrahne [a-teh-kwa-ráh-ne'] on the table
    ennitskwàra chair
        ennitskwahrahne [en-nits-kwa-ráh-ne'] on the chair

Some speakers will say *atehkwahràne* [a-teh-kwa-hrà:-ne'] and *ennitskwahràne* [en-nits-kwa-hrà:-ne'] instead of those shown above.

-akon is a locative that interprets as *in*, or *within*. In some cases it may also be interpreted as *inside*.

> *kanonhsa* house
>> *kanonhsakon* [ka-nónh-sa-konh] in the house
> *onhwentsya* ground
>> *onhwentsyakon* [on-hwén-tsya-konh] in the ground
> *kahyatonhsera* book
>> *kahyatonhserakon* [ka-hya-tonh-se-rá:-konh] in the book
> *ahta'* shoe(s)
>> *ahtahkwakon* [ah-táh-kwa-konh] in the shoe(s)
> *atyàtawi'* coat, shirt, dress
>> *atya'tawi'tsherakon* [a-tya'-ta-wi'ts-he-rá:-konh] in the coat...
> *kerhite* tree
>> *kerhitakon* [ker-hí-ta-konh] within the tree
> *ennitskwàra* chair
>> *ennitskwahratsherakon* [en-nits-kwa-rats-he-rá:-konh]
>>> in the chair

-òkon is a locative that interprets as *under*. In some cases it may also be interpreted as *beneath* or *underneath*.

> *kanonhsa* house
>> *kanonhsòkon* [ka-nonh-sò:-konh] under the house
> *onhwentsya* ground
>> *onhwentsyòkon* [on-hwen-tsyò:-konh] under the ground
> *kerhite* tree
>> *kerhitàke* [ker-hi-tà:-keh] under the tree
> *atehkwàra* table
>> *atehkwahratsheròkon* [a-teh-kwa-hrats-he-rò-konh]
>>> under the table
> *ennitskwàra* chair
>> *ennitskwahratsheròkon* [en-nits-kwa-hrats-he-rò-konh]
>>> under the chair

---

(22)

-akta is a locative that interprets as *beside*. In some cases it may also be interpreted as *near* or *next to*.

kanonhsa house
> *kanonhsakta* [ka-nonh-sák-ta'] near the house

onhwentsya ground
> *onhwentsyakta* [on-hwen-tsyák-ta'] near the ground

kahyatonhsera book
> *kahyatonhserakta* [ka-hya-tonh-se-rák-ta'] near the book

ahta' shoe(s)
> *ahtahkwakta* [ah-tah-kwák-ta'] near the shoe(s)

kerhite tree
> *kerhitakta* [ker-hi-ták-ta'] on / in the tree

atehkwàra table
> *atehkwahratsherakta* [a-teh-kwa-hrats-he-rák-ta']
>> near the table

ennitskwàra chair
> *ennitskwahratsherakta* [en-nits-kwa-hrats-he-rák-ta']
>> near the chair

In the four lists given showing nouns with locative suffixes you will notice that the examples for *table* and *chair* had the connector *-atsher-* whenever a suffix was attached. This is not necessarily always the case. Some speakers will attached the locative suffix directly to the end of the noun after the nominal suffix has bee deleted.

atehkwahrakon [a-teh-kwa-hrá:-konh] inside the table
atehkwahròkon [a-teh-kwa-hrò:-konh] under the table
atehkwahrakta [a-teh-kwa-hrák-ta'] near the table

ennitskwahrakon [en-nits-kwa-hrá:-konh] inside the chair
ennitskwahròkon [en-nits-kwa-hrò:-konh] under the chair
ennitskwahrakta [en-nits-kwa-hrák-ta'] near the chair

SHOWING POSSESSION

Describing the ownership or possession of an object requires use of a prefix that indicates a relationship between the noun and the gender of the individual (owner) involved. There are two sets of prefixes that may be used depending upon whether the noun begins with *a* or a consonant.

SET I.

Atyàtawi' is a noun that begins with *a*. Listed below is the set of prefixes that you would use to show possession.

akw-	*akwatyàtawi'* [a-kwa-tyà:-ta-wi'] my coat
s-	*satyàtawi'* [sa-tyà:-ta-wi'] your coat
rao-	*raotyàtawi'* [ra-o-tyà:-ta-wi'] his coat
akao-	*akaotyàtawi'* [a-ka-o-tyà:-ta-wi'] her coat
ao-	*aotyàtawi'* [a-o-tyà:-ta-wi'] it's coat
onky-	*onkyatyàtawi'* [on-kya-tyà:-ta-wi'] * our coat (two of us)
tsy-	*tsyatyàtawi'* [tsya-tyà:-ta-wi'] * your coat (two of you)
onkw-	*okwatyàtawi'* [on-kwa-tyà:-ta-wi'] * our coat
sew-	*sewatyàtawi'* [se-wa-tyà:-ta-wi'] * your coat (all of you)
raon-	*raonatyàtawi'* [ra-o-na-tyà:-ta-wi'] * their coat (males)
aon-	*aonatyàtawi'* [a-o-na-tyà:-ta-wi'] * their coat (female)

SET II.

kanonhsa is a noun that begins with a consonant. Listed below is the set of prefixes that you would use to show possession.

ake-	*akenonhsa* [a-ke-nónh-sa'] my house
sa-	*sanonhsa* [sa-nónh-sa'] your house
rao-	*raononhsa* [ra-o-nónh-sa'] his house
akao-	*akaononhsa* [a-ka-o-nónh-sa'] her house
ao-	*aononhsa* [a-o-nónh-sa'] it's house

(24)

onkeni-	*onkeninonhsa* [on-ke-ni-nónh-sa'] * our house (two of us)
seni-	*seninonhsa* [se-ni-nónh-sa'] * your house (two of you)
onkwa-	*okwanonhsa* [on-kwa-nónh-sa'] * our house (all of us)
sewa-	*sewanonhsa* [se-wa-nónh-sa'] * your house (all of you)
raoti-	*raotinonhsa* [ra-o-ti-nónh-sa'] * their house (males)
aoti-	*aotinonhsa* [a-o-ti-nónh-sa'] * their house (female)

Note: The possessive prefix *ake-* *'my'* will be reduced to *ak-* when used with noun that begin with *-h* or *-y* (after the nominal prefix is deleted). For example: *akhyatonhsera* [ak-hya-tónh-se-ra'] *'my book'*, or *akyenthohsera* [ak-yent-hóh-se-ra'] *'my (garden) plant'*.

Possessives marked with * indicate that the article under discussion is owned collectively. To refer to individual ownership within the group the suffix *-okon* (as well as any necessary connectors) is used. The accent of the word occur on the suffix.

SET I

onkyatya'tawi'tshera'okon [on-kya-tya'-ta-wi'ts-he-ra'-ó:-konh]
                our coats (one for each of us)
tsyatya'tawi'tshera'okon [tsya-tya'-ta-wi'ts-he-ra'-ó:-konh]
                your coats (one for each of you)

okwatya'tawi'tshera'okon [on-kwa-tya'-ta-wi'ts-he-ra'-ó:-konh]
                our coats (one for each of us)
sewatya'tawi'tshera'okon [se-wa-tya'-ta-wi'ts-he-ra'-ó:-konh]
                your coats (one for each of you)
raonatya'tawi'tshera'okon [ra-o-na-tya'-ta-wi'ts-he-ra'-ó:-konh]
                their coats (one for each of the men)
aonatya'tawi'tshera'okon [a-o-na-tya'-ta-wi'ts-he-ra'-ó:-konh]
                their coats (one for each of the women)

SET II

onkeninonhsa'okon [on-ke-nonh-sa'-ó:-konh]
                our houses (one for each of us)

seninonhsa'okon [se-ni-nonh-sa'-ó:-konh]
your houses (one for each of you)

okwanonhsa'okon [on-kwa-nonh-sa'-ó:-konh]
our houses (one for each of us)

sewanonhsa'okon [se-wa-nonh-sa'-ó:-konh]
your houses (one for each of you)

raonanonhsa'okon [ra-o-ti-nonh-sa'-ó:-konh]
their houses (one for each of the men)

aonanonhsa'okon [a-o-ti-nonh-sa'-ó:-konh]
their houses (one for each of the women)

The preceding examples could also be interpreted as "more than one per individual." For example, *raotinonhsa'okon 'their houses'* could refer to *each individual having a house,* or *having more than one house.*

Attaching suffix *-okon* to the possessive form referring to individuals creates a reference to possession of more than one of the object.

akwatya'tawi'tshera'okon [a-kwa-tya'ta-wi'ts-he-ra'-ó:-konh] my coats
akenonhsa'okon [a-ke-nonh-sa'-ó:-konh] my houses

satya'tawi'tshera'okon [sa-tya'ta-wi'ts-he-ra'-ó:-konh] your coats
sanonhsa'okon [sa-nonh-sa'-ó:-konh] your houses

raotya'tawi'tshera'okon [ra-o-tya'ta-wi'ts-he-ra'-ó:-konh] his coats
raononhsa'okon [ra-o-nonh-sa'-ó:-konh] his houses

akaotya'tawi'tshera'okon [a-ka-o-tya'ta-wi'ts-he-ra'-ó:-konh] her coats
akaononhsa'okon [a-ka-o-nonh-sa'-ó:-konh] her houses

aotya'tawi'tshera'okon [a-o-tya'ta-wi'ts-he-ra'-ó:-konh] its coats
aononhsa'okon [a-o-nonh-sa'-ó:-konh] its houses

Using the vocabulary that you have learned so far practice attaching the appropriate possessive prefixes and, where necessary, the *-okon* suffix. Remember to shift the accent on the words you are using when attaching the *-okon* suffix. Its accent is always consistent.

On the previous pages we have been learning about the possessive. The possessive prefixes can be attached to any word considered inanimate (non-living), but are NEVER USED WITH ANIMATE NOUNS. The notion behind this is the cultural view that it is not possible to own or possess a living creature. Therefore, in Mohawk, to say *my dog* one has to use the patterns shown below.

aketshenen erhar [a-kets-hé:-nen ér-har] my dog
satshenen erhar [sats-hé:-nen ér-har] your dog
raotshenen erhar [ra-ots-hé:-nen ér-har] his dog
akaotshenen erhar [a-ka-ots-hé:-nen ér-har] her dog
aotshenen erhar [a-ots-hé:-nen ér-har] its dog

onkenitshenen erhar [on-ke-nits-hé:-nen ér-har] our dog (two of us)
senitshenen erhar [se-nits-hé:-nen ér-har] your dog (two of you)

onkwatshenen erhar [on-kwats-hé:-nen ér-har] our dog (all of us)
sewatshenen erhar [se-wats-hé:-nen ér-har] your dog (all of you)
raotitshenen erhar [ra-o-tits-hé:-nen ér-har] their dog (males)
aotitshenen erhar [a-o-tits-hé:-nen ér-har] their dog (females)

In a similar way, when talking about *having an animal* a phrase related the verb *-yen' have* is used. For example, one could never say *erhar wakyen' I have a dog.* The following form must be used.

erhar wakenahskwayen' [ér-har wa-ke-náhs-kwa-yen'] I have a dog.
erhar sanahskwayen' [ér-har sa-náhs-kwa-yen'] you have a dog.
erhar ronahskwayen' [ér-har ro-náhs-kwa-yen'] he have a dog.
erhar yakonahskwayen' [ér-har ya-ko-náhs-kwa-yen'] she have a dog.

erhar rotinahskwayen' [ér-har ro-ti-náhs-kwa-yen'] they (M.) have a dog.
erhar yotinahskwayen' [ér-har yo-ti-náhs-kwa-yen'] they (F.) have a dog.

MAKING PLURALS

Describing a noun as being more than just a 'single' or 'individual' in number requires the attachment of suffixes *-okon*, *-okonha*, *hsonha*, or *-hson*. You have already had some experience with the first one when learning about possessives. There are specific uses for each of the *plural suffixes* shown above. The first two, *-okon* and *-okonha*, are used to distinguish between inanimate (non-living) and animate (living) nouns.

Inanimate nouns use the suffix *-okon*.

kanakta bed	*kanakta'okon* [ka-nak-ta'-ó:-konh] beds
kanata town	*kanata'okon* [ka-na-ta'-ó:-konh] towns
kanonhsa house	*kanonhsa'okon* [ka-nonh-sa'-ó:-konh] houses
àthere basket	*a'there'okon* [a'-the-re'-ó:-konh] baskets

Animate nouns use the suffix *-okonha*.

otsitsya flower	*otsi'tsya'okonha*[o-tsi'-tsya'-o-kón-ha'] flowers
otsi'tenha bird	*otsi'tenhokonha* [o-tsi'-ten-ho-kón-ha'] birds
kentsyonk fish	*kentsyonkhokonha* [ken-tsyonk-ho-kón-ha'] fish
erhar dog	*erharhokonha* [er-har-ho-kón-ha'] dogs

The animate suffix *-okonha* will also occur as *-okon'a* in situations of emphasis in some dialects, and almost exclusively as the plural form in other dialects.

otsi'tsya'okon'a [o-tsi'-tsya'-o-kón:-ah] flowers

Not all animate nouns will use the *-okonha* suffix. Some, such as those listed below, require a change in the nominal prefix. The clue to distingishing these nouns from others is the appearance of *pronominal* prefixes. That is, prefixes other than *ka-*, *a-*, *yo*, ect...

ronkwe [rón:-kwe'] man	*rononkwe* [ro-nón:-kwe'] men
yakonkwe [ya-kón:-kwe'] woman	*kononkwe* [ko-nón:-kwe'] women

And some animate nouns require a combination of both.

raksa'a [rak-sá:-ah] boy *ratiksa'okonha* [ra-tik-sa'-o-kón-ha'] boys
yeksa'a [rak-sá:-ah] girl *kontiksa'okonha* [kon-tik-sa'-o-kón-ha'] girls

Some dialects use the third suffix *-hsonha* exclusively to denote the plural form of nouns, regardless of animate or inanimate designation.

kanaktahsonha [ka-nak-tah-són-ha'] beds
otsi'tsyahsonha [o-tsi'-tsyah-són-ha'] flowers
ratiksa'sonha [ra-tik-sa'-són-ha'] boys

In most cases the *-hsonha* suffix may also occur as *-hson'a*.

kanaktahson'a [ka-nak-tah-són:-ah] beds

In some dialects of Mohawk and moreso with some speakers or family groups the use of *-okon / -okonha* and *-hsonha* suffixes designate differences or similarities within the pluralized group.

kahyatonhsera'okon [ka-hya-tonh-se-ra'-ó:-konh] *books*
(refers to a grouping of books which may be all the same size, type, topic, etc...)

kahyatonhserahsonha [ka-hya-tonh-se-rah-són-ha'] *books*
(refers to a grouping of books which are not all the same size, type, topic, etc...)

The final plural suffix, *-hson*, is used with nouns that have locative suffixes (ie. *on, in, under*). The resulting interpretation occurs similar to the folowing examples.

kanonhsàke on the house
     kanonhsa'kehson [ka-nonh-sa'-kéh-sonh] on the houses
kanonhsakon in the house
     kanonhsakonhson [ka-nonh-sa-kónh-sonh] in the houses
kanonhsòkon under the house
     kanonhso'konhson [ka-nonh-so'-kónh-sonh] under the houses

The examples above may also interpret as: *out on.., out in.., out under...*

MAKING DESCRIPTIONS USING NOUNS

Any speaker can easily create nouns with added descriptive features. These descriptions are referred to as *nominal phrases*. Unlike English which uses individual words to create descriptions, Mohawk uses a variety of prefixes, suffixes, or prefix-suffix combinations to produce simple to elaborate descriptive phrases that, in most cases, may exist as free-standing sentence structures. The following examples entail only a small number of the possible descriptions that can occur in the language, but these are possibly the most commonly used.

-iyo This suffix creates the notion of positive attributes when attached to a noun. The interpretation of its use is often rendered as: *good, beautiful, nice*; or may entail the sense of something being: *useful, handy, acceptable, suitable,* or *appropriate.*

> *kanonhsiyo* [ka-nonh-sí:-yoh] *a good house / a nice house...*
> *kanaktiyo* [ka-nak-tí:-yoh] *a good bed / a suitable bed...*
> *wa'shariyo* [wa'-sha-rí:-yoh] *a good knife / a useful knife...*
> *watya'tawi'thseriyo* [wa-tya'-ta-wi'ts-he-rí:-yoh] *a good coat...*

-aksen This suffix creates the notion of negative attributes when attached to a noun. The interpretation of its use is often rendered as: *bad, poor*; or may entail the sense of something being: *useless, awkward, unacceptable, unsuitable,* or *inappropriate.*

> *kanonhsaksen* [ka-nonh-sák-senh] *a poor house...*
> *kanaktaksen* [ka-nak-ták-senh] *a poor bed / unsuitable bed...*
> *wa'sharaksen* [wa'-sha-rák-senh] *a poor knife / useless knife...*
> *watya'tawi'thseraksen* [wa-tya'-ta-wi'ts-he-rák-senh] *a bad coat...*

> NOTE: Nouns that begin with *a*- will occur as *wa*- when any suffix or prefix is used.

-akayon This suffix creates the notion of oldness when attached to a noun. Its is often rendered as: *old, ancient, archaic.*

> *kanonhsakayon* [ka-nonh-sa-ká:-yonh] *an old house...*
> *kanaktakayon* [ka-nak-ta-ká:-yonh] *an old bed...*
> *wa'sharakayon* [wa'-sha-ra-ká:-yonh] *an old knife...*
> *watya'tawi'tsherakayon* [wa-tya'-ta-wi'ts-he-ra-ká:-yonh] *old coat*

-ase This suffix creates the notion of newness or recentness when attached to a noun. The interpretation may occur as: *new, recent, fresh.*

> *kanonhsase* [ka-nonh-sá:-seh] *an new house...*
> *kanakase* [ka-nak-tá:-seh] *an new bed...*
> *wa'sharase* [wa'-sha-rá:-seh] *an new knife...*
> *watya'tawi'tsherase* [wa-tya'-ta-wi'ts-he-rá:-seh] *new coat*

-owanen This suffix creates the notion of largeness when attached to a noun, that is, the object is considered to be *large* because of the way it naturally occurs. It is often rendered as: *big, large, great, etc...*

> *kanonhsowanen* [ka-nonh-so-wá:-nenh] *an big house...*
> *kanaktowanen* [ka-nak-to-wá:-nenh] *an big bed...*
> *wa'sharowanen* [wa'-sha-ro-wá:-nenh] *an big knife...*
> *watya'tawi'tsherowanen* [wa-tya'-ta-wi'ts-he-ro-wá:-nenh] *big coat*

There is another suffix that is often used that also creates a sense of bigness. Suffix *-kowa* is used when the object being spoken of is *big* for the kind of thing it is and not because of its nature.

ni-a'a This suffix creates the notion of smallness when attached to a noun. It may interpret as: *small, little, tiny, etc...*

> *nikanonhsa'a* [ni-ka-nonh-sá:-ah] *an small house...*
> *nikanakta'a* [ni-ka-nak-tá:-ah] *an small bed...*
> *niwa'shara'a* [ni-wa'-sha-rá:-ah] *an small knife...*
> *niwatya'tawi'tshera'a* [ni-wa-tya'-ta-wi'ts-he-rá:-ah] *a small coat*

OWENNAHSON'A

The following is an alphabetical (English) listing of the vocabulary that has appeared in this book.

a'there'okon [a'-the-re'-ó:-konh] *baskets*

ahsire [áh-si-re'] *blanket*

ahta' [áh-ta'] *shoe(s) / footwear;* *ahtahkwàke* [ah-tah-kwà:-keh] *on the shoe(s); ahtahkwakon* [ah-táh-kwa-konh] *in the shoe(s); ahtahkwakta* [ah-tah-kwák-ta'] *near the shoe(s)*

akaononhsa [a-ka-o-nónh-sa'] *her house; akaononhsa'okon* [a-ka-o-nonh-sa'-ó:-konh] *her houses*

akaotshenen erhar [a-ka-ots-hé:-nen ér-har] *her dog*

akaotyàtawi' [a-ka-o-tyà:-ta-wi'] *her coat; akaotya'tawi'tshera'okon* [a-ka-o-tya'ta-wi'ts-he-ra'-ó:-konh] *her coats*

akenonhsa [a-ke-nónh-sa'] *my house; akenonhsa'okon* [a-ke-nonh-sa'-ó:-konh] *my houses*

aketshenen erhar [a-kets-hé:-nen ér-har] *my dog*

akhyatonhsera [ak-hya-tónh-se-ra'] *my book*

akwatyàtawi' [a-kwa-tyà:-ta-wi'] *my coat; akwatya'tawi'tshera'okon* [a-kwa-tya'ta-wi'ts-he-ra'-ó:-konh] *my coats*

akyenthohsera [ak-yent-hóh-se-ra']

my (garden) plant

aonatyàtawi' [a-o-na-tyà:-ta-wi'] *their coat (female);*

aonatya'tawi'tshera'okon [a-o-na-tya'-ta-wi'ts-he-ra'-ó:-konh] *their coats (women)*

aononhsa [a-o-nónh-sa'] *it's house; aononhsa'okon* [a-o-nonh-sa'-ó:-konh] *its houses*

aotinonhsa [a-o-ti-nónh-sa'] *their house (F); aotinonhsa'okon* [a-o-ti-nonh-sa'-ó:-konh] *their houses (F)*

aotitshenen erhar [a-o-tits-hé:-nen ér-har] *their dog (females)*

aotshenen erhar [a-ots-hé:-nen ér-har] *its dog*

aotyàtawi' [a-o-tyà:-ta-wi'] *it's coat; aotya'tawi'tshera'okon* [a-o-tya'ta-wi'ts-he-ra'-ó:-konh] *its coats*

arhya [ár-hya'] *hook / fishhook*

àshare [à:s-ha-reh] *knife;* *wa'sharakayon* [wa'-sha-ra-ká:-yonh] *an old knife; wa'sharaksen* [wa'-sha-rák-senh] *a poor knife; wa'sharase* [wa'-sha-rá:-seh] *an new knife; wa'shariyo* [wa'-sha-rí:-yoh] *a good knife; wa'sharowanen* [wa'-sha-ro-wá:-nenh] *an big knife; niwa'shara'a* [ni-wa'-sha-rá:-ah] *a small knife*

atehkwàra [a-teh-kwà:-ra'] *table;*
atehkwahrahne [a-teh-kwa-ráh-ne']
on the table; atehkwahrakon [a-teh-
kwa-hrá:-konh] *inside the table;*
atehkwahrakta [a-teh-kwa-hrák-ta']
near the table or *atehkwahratshe-*
rakta [a-teh-kwa-hrats-he-rák-ta']
near the table; atehkwahratsheròkon
[a-teh-kwa-hrats-he-rò-konh] *under*
the table or *atehkwahròkon* [a-teh-
kwa-hrò:-konh] *under the table*

àthere [à:-the-reh] *basket*

atoken' [a-tó:-ken'] *axe / hatchet*

atyàtawi' [a-tyà:-ta-wi'] *coat, dress,*
etc...; atya'tawi'tsheràke [a-tya'-ta-
wi'ts-he-rà:-keh] *on the coat...;*
atya'tawi'tsherakon [a-tya'-ta-wi'ts-
he-rá:-konh] *in the coat...; watya'ta-*
wi'thseraksen [wa-tya'-ta-wi'ts-he-
rák-senh] *a bad coat...; watya'ta-*
wi'tsheriyo [wa-tya'-ta-wi'ts-he-rí:-
yoh] *a good coat...; watya'tawi'ts-*
herakayon [wa-tya'-ta-wi'ts-he-ra-
ká:-yonh] *old coat; watya'tawi'ts-*
herase [wa-tya'-ta-wi'ts-he-rá:-seh]
new coat; watya'tawi'tsherowanen
[wa-tya'-ta-wi'ts-he-ro-wá:-nenh] *big*
coat; niwatya'tawi'tshera'a [ni-wa-
tya'-ta-wi'ts-he-rá:-ah] *a small coat*

aweryahsa [a-wer-yáh-sa'] *heart*

ehsa [éh-sa'] *black ash (tree)*

ennitskwàra [en-nits-kwà:-ra'] *chair;*
ennitskwahrahne [en-nits-kwa-ráh-ne']
on the chair; ennitskwahrakon [en-
nits-kwa-hrá:-konh] *inside the chair;*
ennitskwahratsherakon [en-nits-kwa-
rats-he-rá:-konh] *inside the chair;*

ennitskwahratsherakta [en-nits-kwa-
hrats-he-rák-ta'] *beside the chair* or
ennitskwahrakta [en-nits-kwa-hrák-
ta'] *beside the chair; ennitskwa-*
hratsheròkon [en-nits-kwa-hrats-he-
rò-konh] *under the chair* or
ennitskwahròkon [en-nits-kwa-hrò:-
konh] *under the chair*

erhar [ér-har] *dog; erharhokonha* [er-
har-ho-kón-ha'] *dogs*

eryahsa [er-yáh-sa'] *heart*

kahonweya [ka-hon-wé:-ya'] *boat,*
ship, punt, rowboat

kahyatonhsera [ka-hya-tónh-se-ra']
book (it is of a written nature);
kahyatonhseràke [ka-hya-tonh-se-
rà:-keh] *on the book; kahyatonh-*
serakon [ka-hya-tonh-se-rá:-konh] *in*
the book; kahyatonhserakta [ka-hya-
tonh-se-rák-ta'] *near the book*

kanakta [ka-nák-ta'] *bed / place (area,*
space); kanakta'okon [ka-nak-ta'-ó:-
konh] *beds; kanaktahsonha* [ka-nak-
tah-són-ha'] *beds; kanaktakayon* [ka-
nak-ta-ká:-yonh] *an old bed;*
kanaktaksen [ka-nak-ták-senh] *a*
poor bed; kanaktase [ka-nak-tá:-seh]
an new bed; kanaktiyo [ka-nak-tí:-
yoh] *a good bed; kanaktowanen* [ka-
nak-to-wá:-nenh] *a big bed; nikanak-*
ta'a [ni-ka-nak-tá:-ah] *a small bed*

kanata [ka-ná:-ta'] *town, village,*
hamlet, city; kanata'okon [ka-na-ta'-
ó:-konh] *towns*

kanonhsa [ka-nónh-sa'] *house;*
kanonhsa'okon [ka-nonh-sa'-ó:-konh]
houses; kanonhsa'kehson [ka-nonh-

sa'-kéh-sonh] *on the houses*;
kanonhsakayon [ka-nonh-sa-ká:-yonh] *an old house...*; *kanonhsàke* [ka-nonh-sà:-keh] *on the house*; *kanonhsakon* [ka-nónh-sa-konh] *in the house*; *kanonhsakonhson* [ka-nonh-sa-kónh-sonh] *in the houses*; *kanonhsaksen* [ka-nonh-sák-senh] *a poor house*; *kanonhsakta* [ka-nonh-sák-ta'] *near the house*; *kanonhsase* [ka-nonh-sá:-seh] *an new house*; *kanonhsiyo* [ka-nonh-sí:-yoh] *a good house*; *kanonhso'konhson* [ka-nonh-so'-kónh-sonh] *under the houses*; *kanonhsòkon* [ka-nonh-sò:-konh] *under the house*; *kanonhsowanen* [ka-nonh-so-wá:-nenh] *a big house*; *nikanonhsa'a* [ni-ka-nonh-sá:-ah] *a small house...*

karonta [ka-rón:-ta'] *log, tree*

katshe' [káts-he'] *bottle / flask / jar*

kentsyonk [kén-tsyonk] *fish*; *kentsyonkhokonha* [ken-tsyonk-ho-kón-ha'] *fish*

kerhite [kér-hi-te'] *tree*; *kerhitàke* [ker-hi-tà:-keh] *in the tree*; *kerhi'tòkon* [ker-hi'-tò:-konh] *under the tree*; *kerhitakon* [ker-hí-ta-konh] *within the tree*; *kerhitakta* [ker-hi-ták-ta'] *near the tree*

kiken [kí:-ken'] *this (one)* ie. *kiken' kahyatonhsera* [kí:-ken' ka-hya-tónh-se-ra'] *this book*

kononkwe [ko-nón:-kwe'] *women*

kontiksa'okonha [kon-tik-sa'-o-kón-ha'] *girls*

o'nikònra [o'-ni-kòn:-ra'] *spirit / mind /*

consciousness

oh nahòten [oh na-hò:-ten'] *what (is it)?* ie. *Oh nahòten ne'e thiken'* [Oh na-hò:-ten' né:-'eh thí:-ken'] *What is that (thing)?*; *Oh nahòten ne'e kiken'* [Oh na-hò:-ten' né:-'eh kí:-ken'] *What is this (thing)?*

ohonte [ó-hon-te'] *grass/herbs/green*

ohsina [oh-sí:-na'] *leg*

okonhsa [o-kónh-sa'] *face / visage*

onenhste [ó:-nenhs-teh] *corn*

onhwentsya [onh-wén-tsya'] *earth, land, ground*; *onhwentsyàke* [on-hwen-tsyà:-keh] *on the ground*; *onhwentsyakon* [on-hwén-tsya-konh] *in the ground*; *onhwentsyakta* [on-hwen-tsyák-ta'] *near the ground*; *onhwentsyòkon* [on-hwen-tsyò:-konh] *under the ground*

onkeninonhsa [on-ke-ni-nónh-sa'] *our house (two of us)*; *onkeninonhsa'okon* [on-ke-nonh-sa'-ó:-konh] *our houses (one for each of us)*

onkenitshenen erhar [on-ke-nits-hé:-nen ér-har] *our dog (two of us)*

onkwanonhsa [on-kwa-nónh-sa'] *our house (all of us)*; *onkwanonhsa'okon* [on-kwa-nonh-sa'-ó:-konh] *our houses (one for each of us)*

onkwatshenen erhar [on-kwats-hé:-nen ér-har] *our dog (all of us)*

onkwatyàtawi' [on-kwa-tyà:-ta-wi'] *our coat*; *onkwatya'tawi'tshera'okon* [on-kwa-tya'-ta-wi'ts-he-ra'-ó:-konh] *our coats (one for each of us)*

onkyatyàtawi' [on-kya-tyà:-ta-wi'] *our*

coat (two of us);

onkyatya'tawi'tshera'okon [on-kya-tya'-ta-wi'ts-he-ra'-ó:-konh] our coats (one for each of us)

oriwa [o-rí:-wa'] business, matter, deal, word, fault.

oryènta [or-yèn:-ta'] manner, habit, way of doing

otsi'tenha [o-tsi'-tén-ha'] bird; otsi'tenhokonha [o-tsi'-ten-ho-kón-ha'] birds

otsitsya [o-tsì:-tsya'] flower / blossom; otsi'tsya'okonha [o-tsi'-tsya'-o-kón-ha'] flowers or otsi'-tsyahsonha [o-tsi'-tsyah-són-ha'] flowers

owenna [o-wén:-na'] word/voice/tone

oweyenna [o-we-yén:-na'] ability / control / aptitude

owira [o-wí:-ra'] baby

rake'niha [ra-ke'-ní-ha'] my father

raksa'a [rak-sá:-'a] boy; ratiksa'okonha [ra-tik-sa'-o-kón-ha'] boys or ratiksa'sonha [ra-tik-sa'-són-ha'] boys

raktsi'a [rak-tsí:-'a] my older brother

raonatyàtawi' [ra-o-na-tyà:-ta-wi'] their coat (M); raonatya'tawi'tshera'-okon [ra-o-na-tya'-ta-wi'ts-he-ra'-ó:-konh] their coats (one for each)

raononhsa [ra-o-nónh-sa'] his house; raononhsa'okon [ra-o-nonh-sa'-ó:-konh] his houses

raotinonhsa [ra-o-ti-nónh-sa'] their house (males)

raotitshenen erhar [ra-o-tits-hé:-nen ér-har] their dog (males)

raotshenen erhar [ra-ots-hé:-nen ér-har] his dog

raotyàtawi' [ra-o-tyà:-ta-wi'] his coat; raotya'tawi'tshera'okon [ra-o-tya'ta-wi'ts-he-ra'-ó:-konh] his coats

rarihstaherha [ra-rihs-ta-hér-ha'] steel worker

ratiksa'okonha [ra-tik-sa'-o-kón-ha'] boys or ratiksa'sonha [ra-tik-sa'-són-ha'] boys

ratorats [ra-tó:-rats] hunter

rayenthos [ra-yént-hos] farmer

rohninonh [roh-ní:-nonh] he bought

ronahskwayen' [ro-náhs-kwa-yen'] he have an (animal)...

ronatya'atawi'tsherahninonh [ro-na-ka-tya'-ta-wi'ts-he-rah-ní:-nonh] They bought coats.

ronenhstahninonh [ro-nenhs-tah-ní:-nonh] He bought corn.

ronkwe [rón:-kwe'] man; rononkwe [ro-nón:-kwe'] men

rononkwe [ro-nón:-kwe'] men

rotihninonh [ro-tih-ní:-nonh] they bought

rotinahskwayen' [ro-ti-náhs-kwa-yen'] they (M.) have an (animal)...

rotinenhstahninonh [ro-ti-nenhs-tah-ní:-nonh] They bought corn.

rotiyen' [ro-ti':-yen'] they have

rotya'atawi'tsherahninonh [ro-tya'-ta-wi'ts-he-rah-ní:-nonh] He bought a coat.

royen' [ró:-yen'] *he has*

sahninonh [sah-nf:-nonh] *you bought*

sanahskwayen' [sa-náhs-kwa-yen']
you have an (animal)...

sanenhstahninonh [sa-nenhs-tah-nf:-
nonh] *You bought corn.*

sanonhsa [sa-nónh-sa'] *your house;*
sanonhsa'okon [sa-nonh-sa'-ó:-konh]
your houses

satshenen erhar [sats-hé:-nen ér-har]
your dog

satya'tawi'tsherahninonh [sa-tya'tawi'ts-he-rah-nf:-nonh] *You bought a
coat.*

satyàtawi' [sa-tyà:-ta-wi'] *your coat;*
satya'tawi'tshera'okon [sa-tya'tawi'ts-he-ra'-ó:-konh] *your coats*

sayen' [sá:-yen'] *you have*

seninonhsa [se-ni-nónh-sa'] *your
house (two of you); seninonhsa'-
okon* [se-ni-nonh-sa'-ó:-konh] *your
houses (one for each of you)*

senitshenen erhar [se-nits-hé:-nen ér-
har] *your dog (two of you)*

sewanonhsa [se-wa-nónh-sa'] *your
house (all of you); sewanonhsa'okon*
[se-wa-nonh-sa'-ó:-konh] *your
houses (one for each of you)*

sewatshenen erhar [se-wats-hé:-nen
ér-har] *your dog (all of you)*

sewatyàtawi' [se-wa-tyà:-ta-wi'] *your
coat (all of you); sewatya'tawi'tshera'okon* [se-wa-tya'-ta-wi'ts-he-
ra'-ó:-konh] *your coats (one for each
of you)*

shakorihonnyennis [sha-ko-ri-hon-
nyén:-nis] *teacher (male)*

shakoyenahs [sha-ko-yé:-nahs]
policeman

thiken' [thf:-ken'] *that (one)* ie. *thiken'
kahyatonhsera* [thf:-ken' ka-hya-
tónh-se-ra'] *that book*

tsi yontaterihonnyennitha [tsi yon-ta-
te-ri-hon-nyen-nì:t-ha'] *school*

tsi yontenhninonhtha [tsi yon-tenh-ni-
nónht-ha'] *store*

tsi yekhonnyàtha [tsi yek-hon-nyà:-
tha'] *kitchen*

tsyatyàtawi' [tsya-tyà:-ta-wi'] *your
coat (two of you);*

tsyatya'tawi'tshera'okon [tsya-tya'-ta-
wi'ts-he-ra'-ó:-konh] *your coats (one
for each of you)*

wahkwennyatsherarahkwa [wah-
kwen-nyats-he-ra-ráh-kwa'] *clothes
basket / hamper*

wakahsirayen' [wa-kah-si-rá:-yen'] *I
have a blanket.*

wakahtahkwayen' [wa-kah-táh-kwa-
yen'] *I have shoes.*

wakatya'atawi'tsherahninonh [wa-ka-
tya'-ta-wi'ts-he-rah-nf:-nonh] *I
bought a coat.*

wakatya'tawi'tsherayen' [wa-ka-tya'-
ta-wi'ts-he-rá:-yen'] *I have a coat.*

wakenahskwayen' [wa-ke-náhs-kwa-
yen'] *I have an (animal)...*

wakenenhstahninonh [wa-ke-nenhs-
tah-nf:-nonh] *I bought corn*

wakenenhstayen' [wa-ke-nénhs-ta-yen'] *I have corn.*

wakenonhsayen' [wa-ke-nónh-sa-yen'] *I have a house.*

wakhninonh [wak-hnĭ:-nonh] *I bought*

wakhwihstayen' [wak-hwĭhs-ta-yen'] *I have money.*

wakhyatonhserayen' [wak-hya-tonh-se-rá:-yen'] *I have a book.*

wakyen' [wák-yen'] *I have*

yakohninonh [ya-koh-nĭ:-nonh] *she bought*

yakonahskwayen' [ya-ko-náhs-kwa-yen'] *she have an (animal)...*

yakonenhstahninonh [ya-ko-nenhs-tah-nĭ:-nonh] *She bought corn.*

yakonkwe [ya-kón:-kwe'] *woman;* **kononkwe** [ko-nón:-kwe'] *women*

yakotya'tawi'tsherahninonh [ya-ko-tya'ta-wi'ts-he-rah-nĭ:-nonh] *She bought a coat.*

yakoyen' [ya-kó:-yen'] *she has*

yekhsoharehtahkwa [yek-hso-ha-reh-táh-kwa'] *dish cloth*

yekhsokewàtha [yek-hso-ke-wà:-tha'] *tea towel*

yeksa'a [yek-sá:-'a] *girl;* **kontiksa'-okonha** [kon-tik-sa'-o-kón-ha] *girls*

yetsi'tsyarahkwa [ye-tsi'-tsya-ráh-kwa'] *flower vase / pot*

yonatya'tawi'tsherahninonh [yo-na-tya'ta-wi'ts-he-rah-nĭ:-nonh] *They bought coats.*

yononhsa'tariha'tahkwa [yo-nonh-sa'-ta-ri-ha'-táh-kwa'] *stove / heater*

yontorihshentahkwa [yon-to-rihs-hen-táh-kwa'] *sofa / chesterfield*

yotihninonh [yo-tih-nĭ:-nonh] *they bought*

yotinahskwayen' [yo-ti-náhs-kwa-yen'] *they (F.) have an (animal)...*

yotinenhstahninonh [yo-ti-nenhs-tah-nĭ:-nonh] *They bought corn.*

yotiyen' [yo-tĭ:-yen'] *they have*

Part 3

CONTENTS

* * * * * * * * *

PRONUNCIATION

The Mohawk language, represented by this writing system, uses twelve (12) letters (a, h, i, k, n, o, r, s, t, w, y) and a symbol to represent the glottal -'- (also considered to be a consonant). For a more in-depth description of pronunciation see Book 1.

Vowel		Pronunciation	English	Notes
a	ahta	[áh-ta']	shoe	like a in father'
e	wàke'	[wà:-ke']	I'm going	like e in 'they'
	kàsere'	[kà:-se-re']	car	like e in 'met'
i	ise	[í:-se']	you	like ee in 'see'
o	ohsera	[óh-se-ra']	year	like o in 'note'
en	owenna	[o-wén:-na']	word	like u in 'sun'
on	ohonhsa	[o-hónh-sa']	ear	like oo in 'soon'

Consonant		Pronunciation	English	Notes
k	kàsere'	[kà:-se-re']	car	like g in 'gate'
	wakthare	[wák-tha-re']	I converse	like k in 'speak'
t	tare'	[tá:-re']	He comes	like d in 'dog'
	katstha'	[káts-tha']	I use	like t in 'take'
n	onen	[ó:-nen']	now	like n in 'now'
r	raksa'a	[rak-sá:'-ah]	boy	like r in 'run'
s	ohsera	[óh-se-ra']	year	like s in 'sun'
	kàsere'	[kà:-se-re']	car	like z in 'zoo'
w	owira	[o-wí:-ra']	baby	like w in 'wind'
y	oyana	[o-yá:-na']	pair	like y in 'yes'

(3)

VERBS: A description

Mohawk verbs occur as self-contained units of description that are, i
most cases, equal to simple sentences in English. A Mohawk verb, c
verb phrase (a more appropriate term), can and often does contai
references to who and what are involved in the action or activity, as we
as how and when the particular activity, action or process takes place

The VERB PHRASE

The Mohawk verb phrase must always consist of two essential parts: th
verb base, and the pronominal prefix. Additional modifiers in the forr
of prefixes and suffixes may also be attached to this verb phrase in orde
to provide more description about the activity, action, or process.

a)   *Khninons.* [K-hní:-nons] *I buy it (something).*

b)   *Ke'serehtahninons.* [Ke'-se-reh-tah-ní:-nons] *I buy a car.*

The VERB BASE

The verb base is that part of the verb phrase that describes the actior
activity, or process with reference to how, or the way in which th
description may take place. The verb base consists of two essenti
parts: the verb root (the actual description of the action, activity, c
process), and the verb ending (which gives some clue as to when th
description takes place). Consider the verb bases shown above.

a)   *-hninons* [-hní:-nons] *the buying of some thing*

b)   *-'serehtahninons* [-'-se-reh-tah-ní:-nons] *the buying of a car*

PRONOMINAL PREFIXES

A pronominal prefix is that part of every verb phrase that tells who c
what is doing the action. They are similar to the English pronouns: ie
pronoun *he* tells you "who" is doing the action. In English it is alway
separate from the verb: ie. *he is going* ("is going" is the verb). Howeve

in Mohawk the pronominals must be attached to the verb to have meaning.

ra- (a pronominal) + *-torats* (*hunts* a verb) = *ratorats/ he hunts*

Pronominal prefixes are required by every Mohawk verb. They are divided into three series, each creating a slightly different meaning.

i) SUBJECTIVE PRONOMINAL SERIES - of pronominals are used when reference is made to some object or thing: ie. *someone → it.*

Khninons. [K-hní:-nons] *I buy it.*

ikkaryas [ik-kár-yas] *I bite it.*

ii) OBJECTIVE PRONOMINAL SERIES - has two purposes. It may be used when some thing or action is directed toward the speaker.

Wakkaryas [Wak-kár-yas] *It bites me.*

The other use occurs when the speaker declares some action or activity as *having been* completed.

Wakhninonh [Wak-hní:-nonh] *I have bought / I did buy it.*

iii) TRANSITIVE PRONOMINAL SERIES - This last series is used when there is reference made to two or more individuals involved in the action or activity: *someone → someone.*

Riyenteri. [Ri-yen-té:-ri'] *I know him.*

Rakyenteri. [Rak-yen-té:-ri'] *he knows me.*

On the following pages you will be given a detailed look at pronominals. They are VERY IMPORTANT and must be learned in order to acquire any real use of the language.

SUBJECTIVE PRONOMINALS

The pronominal prefixes that occur with verb bases which begin with:
k, t, n, w, y, h or *'*.

k- / ke- / ik-	I	*khninons*	*I buy*
teni-	you & I	*tenihninons*	*we buy*
tewa-	you all & I	*tewahninons*	*we buy*
yakeni-	he / she & I	*yakenihninons*	*we buy*
yakwa-	they & I	*yakwahninons*	*we buy*

hs- / se- / s-	you	*shninons*	*you buy*
seni-	two of you	*senihninons*	*you buy*
sewa-	all of you	*sewahninons*	*you buy*

_____ MALES (only)

ra-	he	*rahninons*	*he buys*
ni-	two of them	*nihninons*	*they buy*
rati-	all of them	*ratihninons*	*they buy*

_____ FEMALES (only)

ye-	she / one / they	*yehninons*	*she buys*
keni-	two of them	*kenihninons*	*they buy*
konti-	all of them	*kontihninons*	*they buy*

_____ THINGS or ANIMALS

ka-	it	*kahninons*	*it buys*

The pronominal prefixes used with verb bases that begin with *a*.

ka-	I	**katkahthos**	*I saw*
tya-	you & I	**tyatkahthos**	*we saw*
tewa-	you all & I	**tewatkahthos**	*we saw*
yakya-	he / she & I	**yakyatkahthos**	*we saw*
yakwa-	they & I	**yakwatkahthos**	*we saw*
sa-	you	**satkahthos**	*you saw*
tsya-	two of you	**tsyatkahthos**	*you saw*
sewa-	all of you	**sewatkahthos**	*you saw*

_____ MALES (only)

ra-	he	**ratkahthos**	*he saw*
ya-	two of them	**yatkahthos**	*they saw*
ron-	all of them	**rontkahthos**	*they saw*

_____ FEMALES (only)

yon-	she / someone / they	**yontkahthos**	*she saw*
kya-	two of them	**kyatkahthos**	*they saw*
kon-	all of them	**kontkahthos**	*they saw*

_____ THINGS or THINGS

wa-	it	**watkahthos**	*it saw*

OBJECTIVE PRONOMINALS

The pronominal prefixes that occur with verb bases which begin with:
k, t, n, w, y, h or *'*.

wak- / wake-	I	**wakhninonh**	*I buy*
yonkeni-	you & I	**yonkenihninonh**	*we buy*
yonkwa-	you all & I	**yonkwahninonh**	*we buy*
yonkeni-	he / she & I	**yonkenihninonh**	*we buy*
yonkwa-	they & I	**yonkwahninonh**	*we buy*

sa-	you	**sahninonh**	*you buy*
seni-	two of you	**senihninonh**	*you buy*
sewa-	all of you	**sewahninonh**	*you buy*

_____ MALES (only)

ro-	he	**rohninonh**	*he buys*
roti-	two of them	**rotihninonh**	*they buy*
roti-	all of them	**rotihninonh**	*they buy*

_____ FEMALES (only)

yako-	she / one / they	**yakohninonh**	*she buys*
yoti-	two of them	**yotihninonh**	*they buy*
yoti-	all of them	**yotihninonh**	*they buy*

_____ THINGS or ANIMALS

yo-	it	**yohninonh**	*it buys*

The pronominal prefixes that occur with verb bases beginning with *a*.

waka-	I	*wakatkahthonh*	I did see
yonkya-	you & I	*yonkyatkahthonh*	we did see
yonkwa-	you all & I	*yonkwatkahthonh*	we did see
yonkya-	he / she & I	*yonkyatkahthonh*	we did see
yonkwa-	they & I	*yonkwatkahthonh*	we did see

sa-	you	*satkahthonh*	you did see
tsya-	two of you	*tsyatkahthonh*	you did see
sewa-	all of you	*sewatkahthonh*	you did see

_____ MALES (only)

ro-	he	*rotkahthonh*	he did see
rona-	two of them	*ronatkahthonh*	they did see
rona-	all of them	*ronatkahthonh*	they did see

_____ FEMALES (only)

yako-	she / someone / they	*yakotkahthonh*	she did see
yona-	two of them	*yonatkahthonh*	they did see
yona-	all of them	*yonatkahthonh*	they did see

_____ THINGS or THINGS

yo-	it	*yotkahthonh*	it did see

SPEAKING OF COMPLETED ACTIONS: has / have / did

When the speaker is referring to an activity or action that has been completed, the Perfect sense will be used. Using the Perfect requires the Objective pronominals. These pronominals are most often used in conjunction with an *-h*, or *onh* ending on the verb phrase. The result will interpret as: *has...*, *have...*, or *did....* The arrangement of words is the same as shown with the Subjective examples (page   ).

1)   **Wakatkahthonh ne kàsere'.**   [Wa-kat-káht-honh ne kà:-sere']
I have seen the car / I did see the car.

2)   **Yakotkahthonh ne yeksa'a.**   [Ya-kot-káht-honh ne yek-sá:-'ah]
The girl has seen / The girl did see (it).

3)   **Yonkwatkahthonh thiken' àshare.**
[Yon-kwat-káht-honh thí:-ken' à:-s-ha-reh]
We have seen that knife / We did see that knife.

4)   **Rohninonh kiken' ronkwe.**   [Roh-ní:-nonh kí:-ken' rón:-kwe']
This man has bought / This man did buy (it).

5) **Rotihninonh thiken' kàsere'.**   [Ro-tih-ní:-nonh thí:-ken' kà:-se-re']
They have bought that car / They did buy that car.

6)   **Yotihninonh ne kàsere' kiken' kononkwe.**
[Yo-tih-ní:-nonh ne kà:-se-re' thí:-ken' ko-nón:-kwe']
Those women have bought the car / Those women did buy that car.

7)   **Tawit nok ni'i yonkyatkahthonh thiken' àshare.**
[Tá:-wit nok ní:-'ih yon-kyat-káht-honh thí:-ken' à:-s-ha-reh]
David and I have seen that knife / David and I did see that knife.

8)   **Wari nok ni'i yonkenihninonh kiken' àthere.**
[Wá:-rih nok ní:-'ih yon-ke-nih-ní:-nonh kí:-ken' à:-s-ha-reh]
Mary and I have bought this basket / Mary and I did buy this basket.

9)   *Tawit nok ne Sose ronatkahthonh thiken' kàsere'.*
         [Tá:-wit nok ne Só:-seh ro-nat-káht-honh thí:-ken' kà:-se-re']
         David and Joe have seen that car / David and Joe did see that car.

10)   *Wari nok ne Sose ronatkahthonh kiken' kahonweya.*
         [Wá:-rih nok ne Só:-seh ro-nat-káht-honh kí:-ken' ka-hon-wé:-ya']
         Mary and Joe have seen this boat / Mary and Joe did see this boat.

11)   *Rotihninonh kiken' kàsere' thiken' tehnonkwe.*
         [Ro-tih-ní:-nonh kí:-ken' kà:-se-re' thí:-ken' teh-nón:-kwe']
         Those two men bought / did buy this car.

12)   *Yonatkahthonh ne kahonweya kiken' tekeniksa'a.*
         [Yo-nat-káht-honh ne ka-hon-wé:-ya' kí:-ken' te-ke-nik-sá:-'ah]
         These two girls have seen / did see the boat.

USING *ONEN* TO MAKE *ALREADY* STATEMENTS:
In order to make an *already have* or *have already* statements, the word
onen will appear directly before the verb phrase.

Onen wakhninonh ne kàsere'. [Ó:-nenh wak-hní:-nonh ne kà:-se-re']
         I have already bought the car.

Onen yakohninonh kiken' atyàtawi' ne akokstenha.
[Ó:-nenh ya-koh-ní:-nonh kí:-ken' a-tyà:-ta-wi' ne a-koks-tén-ha']
         The old lady has already bought this coat.

Onen rotkahthonh ne kahonweya thiken' rokstenha.
[Ó:-nenh rot-káht-honh ne ka-hon-wé:-ya' thí:-ken' roks-tén-ha']
         That old man has already seen the boat.

Onen ronatkahthonh kiken' kahonweya ne ratiksa'okonha.
[Ó:-nenh ro-nat-káht-honh kí:-ken' ka-hon-wé:-ya'
                   ne ra-tik-sa'-o-kón-ha']
         The boys have already seen this boat.

TRANSITIVE PRONOMINALS

These prefixes occur with verb bases beginning: **k, t, n, w, y, h** or **'**.

kon-	I → you	**konhroris**	I tell you
kwa-	I → you (all)	**kwahroris**	I tell you (all)
ri-	I → him	**rihroris**	I tell him
khe-	I → her / them	**khehroris**	I tell her / them
tak(e)-	you → me	**takhroris**	you tell me
takwa-	you → us	**takwahroris**	you tell us
etsh(e)-	you → him	**etshroris**	you tell him
she-	you → her / them	**shehroris**	you tell her...
rak(e)-	he → me	**rakhroris**	he tells me
shonkwa-	he → us	**shonkwahroris**	he tells us
ya-	he → you	**yahroris**	he tells you
ro-	he → him	**rohroris**	he tells him
shako-	he → her / them	**shakohroris**	he tells them
yonk(e)-	she → me	**yonkhroris**	she tells me
yonkhi-	she → us	**yonkhihroris**	she tells us
yesa-	she → you	**yesahroris**	she tells you
ronwa-	she → him	**ronwahroris**	she tells him
yontat(e)-	she → her	**yontathroris**	she tells her
ronwati-	she → them	**ronwatihroris**	she tells them

The transitive pronominals used with verb bases beginning with **a**.

konya-	I → you	**konyathroris**	*I tell about you*
kwa-	I → you (all)	**kwathroris**	*I tell...you (all)*
riya-	I → him	**riyathroris**	*I tell...him*
kheya-	I → her / them	**kheyathroris**	*I tell...her/them*

takwa-	you → me	**takwathroris**	*you tell...me*
takwa-	you → us	**takwathroris**	*you tell...us*
etshey-	you → him	**etsheyathroris**	*you tell...him*
sheya-	you → her / them	**sheyathroris**	*you tell...her/...*

rakwa-	he → me	**rakwathroris**	*he tells...me*
shonkwa-	he → us	**shonkwathroris**	*he tells...us*
ya-	he → you	**yathroris**	*he tells...you*
ro-	he → him	**rothroris**	*he tells...him*
shako-	he → her / them	**shakothroris**	*he tells...them*

yonkwa-	she → me	**yonkwathroris**	*she tells...me*
yonkhiya-	she → us	**yonkhiyathroris**	*she tells...us*
yesa-	she → you	**yesathroris**	*she tells...you*
ronwa-	she → him	**ronwathroris**	*she tells...him*
yontata-	she → her	**yontatathroris**	*she tells...her*
ronwana-	she → them	**ronwanathroris**	*she tells...them*

MAKING REFERENCE TO OTHERS

Reference to others will require the Transitive pronominals, which must agree in gender and number with the individuals in question.

Rihroris. [Ri-hró:-ris] *I tell him.*

Rihroris ne raksa'a. [Ri-hró:-ris ne rak-sá:-'ah]
I tell the boy.

Raksa'a, *boy*, refers directly to the *him* of the Transitive pronominal. If the statement is reversed the word arrangement remains the same.

Rakhroris. [Rak-hró:-ris] *He tells me.*

Rakhroris ne raksa'a. [Rak-hró:-ris ne rak-sá:-'ah]
The boy tells me.

In situations of confusion (ambiguity) over who is *doing* the action and who is *receiving*, the word arrangement will occur as follows.

Raksa'a rohroris ne ronkwe'. [Rak-sá:-'ah ro-hró:-ris ne rón:-kwe']
A boy tells the man.

Thiken' yakonkwe yontathroris ne akokstenha.
[Thí:-ken' ya-kón:-kwe' yon-tat-hró:-ris ne a-koks-tén-ha']
That woman tells the old woman.

In most other situations the arrangment of the words will occur the same as shown with the Subjective and the Objective examples.

Ronwahroris ne ronkwe thiken' akokstenha.
[Ron-wa-hró:-ris ne rón:-kwe' thí:-ken' a-koks-tén-ha']
That old woman tells the man.

Shakohroris thiken' yakonkwe ne rokstenha.
[Sha-ko-hró:-ris thí:-ken' ya-kón:-kwe' ne roks-tén-ha']
The old man tells that woman.

ADDITIONAL EXAMPLES for PRACTICE:

1) **_Riyathroris thiken' raksa'a._**
   [Ri-yat-hró:-ris thí:-ken' rak-sá:-'ah]
   I tell about that boy.

2) **_Kheyathroris kiken' yakonkwe._**
   [K-he-yat-hró:-ris kí:-ken' ya-kón:-kwe']
   I tell about this woman.

3) **_Kheyathroris ne tehniksa'a._**
   [K-he-yat-hró:-ris ne teh-nik-sá:-'ah]
   I tell about the two boys.

4) **_Kheyathroris ne tekeniksa'a._**
   [K-he-yat-hró:-ris ne te-ke-nik-sá:-'ah]
   I tell about the two girls.

5) **_Kheyathroris ne ratiksa'okonha._**
   [K-he-yat-hró:-ris ne ra-tik-sa'-o-kón-ha']
   I tell about the boys.

6) **_Kheyathroris thiken' kontiksa'okonha._**
   [K-he-yat-hró:-ris thí:-ken' kon-tik-sa'-o-kón-ha']
   I tell about those girls.

7) **_Rakhroris thiken' rokstenha._**
   [Rak-hró:-ris thí:-ken' roks-tén-ha']
   That old man tells me.

8) **_Yathroris kiken' raksa'taksen._**
   [Yat-hró:-ris kí:-ken' rak-sa'-ták-senh]
   This bad boy tells about you.

9) **_Kiken' rokstenha rohroris ne raksa'taksen._**
   [Kí:-ken' roks-tén-ha' ro-hró:-ris ne rak-sa'-ták-senh]
   This old man tells the bad boy.

10)   ***Shakothroris kiken' akokstenha ne rakenoha'a.***
         [Sha-kot-hró:-ris kí:-ken' a-koks-tén-ha' ne ra-ke-no-há:-'ah]
         My uncle tells about this old woman.

11)   ***Shakohroris thiken' ratiksa'taksen ne ya'niha.***
         [Sha-ko-hró:-ris thí:-ken' ra-tik-sa'-ták-senh ne ya'-ní-ha']
         Your father tells those bad boys.

12)   ***Yonkhroris kiken' akokstenha.***
                [Yonk-hró:-ris kí:-ken' a-koks-tén-ha']
                This old woman tells me.

13)   ***Yonkhroris thiken' rononkwe'tiyos.***
                [Yonk-hró:-ris thí:-ken' ro-non-kwe'-tí:-yos]
                Those good men tell me.

14)   ***Yesathroris thiken' yeksa'taksen.***
                [Ye-sat-hró:-ris thí:-ken' yek-sa'-ták-senh]
                That bad girl tells about you.

15)   ***Kiken' akokstenha yontathroris ne niyaka'ah yeksa'a.***
      [Kí:-ken' a-koks-tén-ha' yon-tat-hró:-ris ne ni-ya-ká:-'ah yek-sá:-'ah]
      This old woman tells the small girl.

16)   ***Ronwathroris kiken' nihra'a raksa'a ne ihsta'a.***
        [Ron-wat-hró:-ris kí:-ken' nihrá:-'ah rak-sá:-'ah ne ihs-tá:-'ah]
        My aunt tells about this small boy.

17)   ***Ronwahroris kiken' nihra'a raksa'a ne kononkwe.***
        [Ron-wat-hró:-ris kí:-ken' nihrá:-'ah rak-sá:-'ah ne ko-nón:-kwe']
        The women tell about this small boy.

18)   ***Ronwatihroris kiken' rononkwe thiken' rotiksten'okonha.***
       [Ron-wa-ti-hró:-ris kí:-ken' ro-nón:-kwe'
       thí:-ken' ro-tik-sten'-o-kón-ha']
       Those old men tell these men.

MODALS

Modals are prefixes attached to verbs that describe the time in which some activity, action, or process took place. In Mohawk there are three such modals: the aorist; the future; and the non-definite.

i) The **AORIST** - This modal prefix often indicates the *immediate past* marker: ie. when the speaker wishes to refer to some activity, action, or process as having been *just* begun, or *just* completed. It is most often used with *temporal* descriptions of time: ie..*yesterday, last night, a week ago, etc...* It most often appears as: **wa´**, **wa**, or **we**.

> **Wa'katkahtho´.** [Wa'-kat-káht-ho'] / *(just) saw it.*

> **Thetenre wahahninon´** [T-he-tén:-reh wa-hah-ní:-non']
> *He bought it yesterday.*

ii) The **FUTURE** - occurring as **en-**, refers to some activity, action, or process that takes place after the point of speaking or reference.   It occurs with *temporal* descriptions such as *tomorrow, next week, etc.*

> **Enyehninon´.** [En-yeh-ní:-non'] *She will buy it.*

> **Enyorhenne´ enyakwahninon´.** [En-yór-hen'-ne' en-ya-kwah-ní:-non']
> *Tomorrow she will buy it.*

iii) The **NON-DEFINITE** - occurring as **a-** is used when the speaker joins two verb phrases together to make a single statement. When it occurs it often interprets as *would, should etc...*

> **Kenònwe's akatorate´.** [Ke-nòn:-we's a-ka-tó:-ra-te']
> *I like to hunt.*

> **Irehre´ ne ayehninon´.** [Í:-reh-re' na-yeh-ní:-non']
> *He wants her to buy it.*

See the following pages for additonal information on the shape and use of the Modals.

USING AORIST MODAL : WA'-

AORIST with verb bases that begin with **k, t, n, w, y, h** or glottal '.

wa'k(e)-	I	**wa'khninon'**	*I bought*
weteni-	you & I	**wetenihninon'**	*we bought*
wetewa-	you all & I	**wetewahninon'**	*we bought*
wa'akeni-	he / she & I	**wa'akenihninon'**	*we bought*
wa'akwa-	they & I	**wa'akwahninon'**	*we bought*

wahs(e)-	you	**wahshninon'**	*you bought*
weseni-	two of you	**wesenihninon'**	*you bought*
wesewa-	all of you	**wesewahninon'**	*you bought*

_____ MALES (only)

waha-	he	**wahahninon'**	*he bought*
wahni-	two of them	**wahnihninon'**	*they bought*
wahati-	all of them	**wahatihninon'**	*they bought*

_____ FEMALES (only)

wa'e-	she / one / they	**wa'ehninon'**	*she bought*
wa'keni-	two of them	**wa'kenihninon'**	*they bought*
wa'konti-	all of them	**wa'kontihninon'**	*they bought*

_____ THINGS or ANIMALS

wa'ka-	it	**wa'kahninon'**	*it bought*

AORIST with verb bases that begin with *a*.

wa'ka-	I	**wa'katkahtho'**	*I saw*
wetya-	you & I	**wetyatkahtho'**	*we saw*
wetewa-	you all & I	**wetewatkahtho'**	*we saw*
wa'akya-	he / she & I	**wa'akyatkahtho'**	*we saw*
wa'akwa-	they & I	**wa'akwatkahtho'**	*we saw*

wehsa-	you	**wehsatkahtho'**	*you saw*
wetsya-	two of you	**wetsyatkahtho'**	*you saw*
wesewa-	all of you	**wesewatkahtho'**	*you saw*

_____ MALES (only)

waha-	he	**wahatkahtho'**	*he saw*
wahya-	two of them	**wahyatkahtho'**	*they saw*
wahon-	all of them	**wahontkahtho'**	*they saw*

_____ FEMALES (only)

wa'on-	she / someone / they	**wa'ontkahtho'**	*she saw*
wa'kya-	two of them	**wa'kyatkahtho'**	*they saw*
wa'kon-	all of them	**wa'kontkahtho'**	*they saw*

_____ THINGS or THINGS

on-	it	**ontkahtho'**	*it saw*

USING FUTURE MODAL: EN-

FUTURE with verb bases that begin with **k, t, n, w, y, h** or glottal ´.

enk-	I	**enkhninon´**	*I will buy*
enteni-	you & I	**entenihninon´**	*we will buy*
entewa-	you all & I	**entewahninon´**	*we will buy*
enyakeni-	he / she & I	**enyakenihninon´**	*we will buy*
enyakwa-	they & I	**enyakwahninon´**	*we will buy*

enhs-	you	**enhshninon´**	*you will buy*
enseni-	two of you	**ensenihninon´**	*you will buy*
ensewa-	all of you	**ensewahninon´**	*you will buy*

_____ MALES (only)

enha-	he	**enhahninon´**	*he will buy*
enhni-	two of them	**enhnihninon´**	*they will buy*
enhati-	all of them	**enhatihninon´**	*they will buy*

_____ FEMALES (only)

enye-	she / someone / they	**enyehninon´**	*she will buy*
enkeni-	two of them	**enkenihninon´**	*they will buy*
enkonti-	all of them	**enkontihninon´**	*they will buy*

_____ THINGS or ANIMALS

enka-	it	**enkahninon´**	*it will buy*

FUTURE with verb bases that begin with *a*.

enka-	I	**enkatkahtho´**	*I will see*
entya-	you & I	**entyatkahtho´**	*we will see*
entewa-	you all & I	**entewatkahtho´**	*we will see*
enyakya-	he / she & I	**enyakyatkahtho´**	*we will see*
enyakwa-	they & I	**enyakwatkahtho´**	*we will see*

enhsa-	you	**enhsatkahtho´**	*you will see*
entsya-	two of you	**entsyatkahtho´**	*you will see*
ensewa-	all of you	**ensewatkahtho´**	*you will see*

_____ MALES (only)

enha-	he	**enhatkahtho´**	*he will see*
enhya-	two of them	**enhyatkahtho´**	*they will see*
enhon-	all of them	**enhontkahtho´**	*they will see*

_____ FEMALES (only)

enyon-	she / someone / they	**enyontkahtho´**	*she will see*
enkya-	two of them	**enkyatkahtho´**	*they will see*
enkon-	all of them	**enkontkahtho´**	*they will see*

_____ THINGS or ANIMALS

enwa-	it	**enwatkahtho´**	*it will see*

USING THE NON-DEFINITE MODAL: A-

NON-DEFINITE with verb bases that begin *k, t, n, w, y, h* or glottal *'*.

ak-	I	**akhninon'**	*I would buy*
aeteni-	you & I	**aetenihninon'**	*we would buy*
aetewa-	you all & I	**aetewahninon'**	*we would buy*
ayakeni-	he / she & I	**ayakenihninon'**	*we would buy*
ayakwa-	they & I	**ayakwahninon'**	*we would buy*

ahs-	you	**ahshninon'**	*you would buy*
aeseni-	two of you	**aesenihninon'**	*you would buy*
aesewa-	all of you	**aesewahninon'**	*you would buy*

_____ MALES (only)

aha-	he	**ahahninon'**	*he would buy*
ahni-	two of them	**ahnihninon'**	*they would buy*
ahati-	all of them	**ahatihninon'**	*they would buy*

_____ FEMALES (only)

aye-	she / someone / they	**ayehninon'**	*she would buy*
akeni-	two of them	**akenihninon'**	*they would buy*
akonti-	all of them	**akontihninon'**	*they would buy*

_____ THINGS or ANIMALS

aka-	it	**akahninon'**	*it would buy*

NON-DEFINITE with verb bases that begin with *a*.

aka-	I	**akatkahtho´**	*I would see*
aetya-	you & I	**aetyatkahtho´**	*we would see*
aetewa-	you all & I	**aetewatkahtho´**	*we would see*
ayakya-	he / she & I	**ayakyatkahtho´**	*we would see*
ayakwa-	they & I	**ayakwatkahttho´**	*we would see*
ahsa-	you	**ahsatkahtho´**	*you would see*
aetsya-	two of you	**aetsyatkahtho´**	*you would see*
aesewa-	all of you	**aesewatkahtho´**	*you would see*

_____ MALES (only)

aha-	he	**ahatkahtho´**	*he would see*
ahya-	two of them	**ahyatkahtho´**	*they would see*
ahon-	all of them	**ahontkahtho´**	*they would see*

_____ FEMALES (only)

ayon-	she / someone / they	**ayontkahtho´**	*she would see*
akya-	two of them	**akyatkahtho´**	*they would see*
akon-	all of them	**akontkahtho´**	*they would see*

_____ THINGS or ANIMALS

aon-	it	**aontkahtho´**	*it would see*

CREATING SENTENCES

Placing words with verbs to create sentences can be an easy process.

Ratkahthos ne raksa'a. [Rat-káh-thos ne rak-sá:-'ah] *The boy sees it.*

Raksa'a refers to only one person, and the pronominal prefix *ra-* indicates a single *male* individual. If the speaker refers to two, or more individuals then the pronominal being used must agree.

> **Yatkahthos ne tehniksa'a.** [Yat-káh-thos ne teh-nik-sá:-'ah]
> *The two boys see (it).*

> **Rontkahthos ne ratiksa'okonha.** [Ront-káh-thos ne ra-tik-sa'-o-kón-ha']
> *The boys see (it).*

The verb being used makes reference to seeing an inanimate object (ie. a thing). If mention is made of some thing, the word used to describe it will occur right after the verb phrase.

> **Ratkahthos ne kàsere'.** [Rat-káh-thos ne kà:-se-re']
> *He sees the car.*

> **Ratkahthos thiken' kàsere'.** [Rat-káh-thos thí:-ken' kà:-se-re']
> *He sees that car.*

When the speaker mentions the one involved in the action as well as some thing or object the word arrangement will be: the verb phrase (with the appropriate pronominal); the thing or object spoken of; and the individual or individuals involved with the action or activity.

> **Ratkahthos thiken' kàsere' ne raksa'a.**
> [Rat-káh-thos thí:-ken' kà:-se-re' ne rak-sá:-'ah]
> *The boy sees that car.*
>
> or
>
> **Ratkahthos ne kàsere' thiken' raksa'a.**
> [Rat-káh-thos ne kà:-se-re' thí:-ken' rak-sá:-'ah]
> *That boy sees the car.*

ADDITIONAL EXAMPLES for PRACTICE:

1)   ***Yehninons ne yeksa'a.*** [Yeh-ní:-nons ne yek-sá:-'ah]
         The girl buys it.

2)   ***Yehninons ne atyàtawi'.*** [Yeh-ní:-nons ne a-tyà:-ta-wi']
         She buys the coat.

3)   ***Yehninons kiken' yeksa'a.*** [Yeh-ní:-nons kí:-ken' yek-sa'ah]
         This girl buys it.

4)   ***Yehninons kiken' àthere ne yeksa'a.***
         [Yeh-ní:-nons kí:-ken' à:-t-he-reh ne yek-sa'ah]
         The girl buys this basket.

5)   ***Yehninons ne àthere kiken' yeksa'a.***
         [Yeh-ní:-nons ne à:-t-he-reh kí:-ken' yek-sa'ah]
         This girl buys it.

6)   ***Ratihninons ne rononkwe'.*** [Ra-tih-ní:-nons ne ro-nón:-kwe']
         The men buy it.

7)   ***Kontihninons ne kontiksa'okonha.***
         [Kon-ti-hní:-nons ne kon-tik-sa'-o-kón-ha']
         The girls buy it.

8)   ***Sewatis nok ni'i yakyatkahthos.***
         [Se-wá-tis nok ní:-'ih ya-kyat-káh-thos]
         John and I see it.

9)   ***Sewatis nok ne Sose yatkahthos.***
         [Se-wá-tis nok ne Só:-seh yat-káh-thos]
         John and Joe see it.

10)   ***Wari tahnon ne Konwakeri kyatkahthos.***
         [Wá-rih nok ne Kon-wá-ke-rih kyat-káh-thos]
         Mary and Margaret see it.

EXAMPLES USING MODALS:

11)   *Wa'ehninon' ne yeksa'a.* [Wa'-eh-ní:-non' ne yek-sá:-'ah]
      The girl bought it.

12)   *Enyehninon' ne atyàtawi'.* [En-yeh-ní:-non' ne a-tyà:-ta-wi']
      She will buy the coat.

13)   *Iyenhre' ayehninon' kiken' àthere ne yeksa'a.*
      [í:-yen-hre' a-yeh-ní:-non' kí:-ken' à:-t-he-reh ne yek-sa'ah]
      The girl wants to buy this basket.

14*Wahatihninon' ne rononkwe'.* [Wa-ha-tih-ní:-non' ne ro-nón:-kwe']
      The men bought it.

15)   *Enkontihninon' ne kiken' kontiksa'okonha.*
      [En-kon-ti-hní:-non' ne kí:-ken' kon-tik-sa'-o-kón-ha']
      These girls will buy it.

16)   *Sewatis nok ni'i Wa'akyatkahtho'.*
      [Se-wá-tis nok ní:-'ih wa'-a-kyat-káh-tho']
      John and I saw it.

17)   *Sewatis nok ne Sose wahyatkahthos.*
      [Se-wá-tis nok ne Só:-seh wa-hyat-káh-thos]
      John and Joe saw it.

18)   *Wari tahnon ne Konwakeri enkyatkahtho'.*
      [Wá-rih nok ne Kon-wá-ke-rih en-kyat-káh-tho']
      Mary and Margaret will see it.

19)   *Inehre' ne Wari nok ne Sose ahyatkahtho' thiken' kàsere'.*
      [Ì:-ne-hre' ne Wá-rih nok ne Só:-seh a-hyat-káh-thos
      ne thí:-ken' kà:-se-re']
      Mary and Joe want to see that car.

(26)

MAKING NEGATIVE STATEMENTS

In any conversation it is occasionally necessary to make a negative statement about some topic, individual, or thing. In Mohawk, the "no" word **yah** is used in conjunction with a **te** verb prefix. The simplest negative statement is of the *"it is not"* variety.

Iken'. [í:-ken'] *It is.*

Yah teken'. [Yah té:-ken'] *It is not.*

If the speaker is making a negative statement about some individual or thing, the topic in question is placed between the **yah** and **te** prefix.

with FREE PRONOUNS

Yah i'i teken'. [Yah í:-'ih té:-ken']
It's not me / I am not the one.

Yah raonha teken'. [Yah rá-on-ha' té:-ken']
It's not him / He is not the one.

Yah akaonha teken'. [Yah a-ká-on-ha' té:-ken']
It's not her / She is not the one.

with DEMONSTRATIVES

Yah kiken' teken'. [Yah kí:-ken' té:-ken']
It's not this / This is not the one.

Yah thiken' teken'. [Yah t-hí:-ken' té:-ken']
It's not that / That is not the one.

with NOMINALS

Yah erhar teken'. [Yah ér-har té:-ken']
It's not a dog / A dog is not the one.

Yah ne raksa'a teken'. [Yah ne rak-sá:-'ah té:-ken']
It's not the boy / The boy is not the one.

In the examples shown on the previous page the topic in question (a nominal, demonstrative phrase, or a free pronoun) occurs between the *yah* and *teken'* phrase. The following pages will show how to expand the negative to include actions, activities, and states.

NEGATIVE with SUBJECTIVE Pronominal prefixes

The *"no"* word *yah* can be used with verbs that require the subjective pronominals (as shown on pages   ) in conjunction with the prefix *te-* is required. Consider the following with English interpretations.

> *Yah tekhninons* [Yah tek-hní:-nons]
> *I don't buy / I'm not a buyer.*

> *Yah tehahninons* [Yah te-hah-ní:-nons]
> *He doesn't buy / He's not a buyer.*

> *Yah teyehninons* [Yah te-yeh-ní:-nons]
> *She doesn't buy / She's not a buyer.*

> *Yah tehatihninons* [Yah te-ha-tih-ní:-nons]
> *They don't buy / They are not buyers.*

> *Yah teyakwahninons* [Yah te-ya-kwah-ní:-nons]
> *We don't buy / We are not buyers.*

If nominals are used in negative constructions, this pattern will occur.

> *Yah tehahninons ne raksa'a.* [Yah te-hah-ní:-nons ne rak-sá:-'ah]
> *The boy doesn't buy / The boy is not a buyer.*

> *Yah teyehninons thiken' yakonkwe.*
>   [Yah te-yeh-ní:-nons thí:-ken' ya-kón;-kwe']
> *That woman doesn't buy / That woman is not a buyer.*

> *Yah tehatihninons kiken' ratiksa'okonha.*
>   [Yah te-ha-tih-ní:-nons kí:-ken' ra-tik-sa'-o-kón:-ha']
> *These boys don't buy / These boys are not buyers.*

NEGATIVE with OBJECTIVE Pronominal prefixes

The negative construction, when used with objective pronominals in stative constructions, also provide *is not / are not* statements.

Yah tewakenonhwaktani [Yah te-wa-ke-non-hwák-ta-nih]
I am not sick.

Yah tehotshennonni [Yah te-hots-hen-nón:-nih]
He is not happy.

Yah teyoti'nikonhraksen [Yah te-yo-ti'-ni-kon-hrák-senh]
They (females) are not sad.

If the Negative with Objective is used with verbs occuring in the Perfect sense, you will get *has not / have not* or *did not* statements.

Yah tewakhninonh [Yah te-wak-hní:-nonh]
I have bought / I did not buy.

Yah teyakotenhninonh [Yah te-ya-ko-tenh-ní:-nonh]
She hasn't sold / She did not sell.

Yah teyonkwatkahthonh [Yah te-yon-kwat-káh-thonh]
We have not seen / We did not see.

Nominals modifying a negative construction will provide the following.

Yah tehotkahthonh thiken' raksa'a.
[Yah te-hot-káh-thonh thí:-ken' rak-sá:-'ah]
That boy hasn't seen / did not see (it).

Yah teyakohninonh kiken' àthere ne yeksa'a.
Yah t-ha-yeh-ní:-nonh kí:-ken' à:-t-he-reh ne yek-sá:-'ah]
The girl hasn't bought / did not buy this basket.

Yah tehotinenhskwenh ne kàsere' thiken' rononkwe.
[Yah te-ho-ti-nénhs-kwenh ne kà:-se-re' thí:-ken' ro-nó:-kwe']
Those men have not stolen / did not steal the car.

NEGATIVE with NON-DEFINITE.

In *won't* or *wouldn't* statements, the negative word *yah* with prefix *th-* is used with non-definite verb constructions (see page   ).

Yah thahakwatako'. [Yah t-ha-ha-kwa-tá:-ko']
    He won't / wouldn't fix (it).

Yah thayekhonni'. [Yah t-ha-yek-hón:-ni']
    She won't / wouldn't cook.

Yah thahakyenawa'se'. [Yah t-ha-kyé:-na-wa'-se']
    He won't / wouldn't help me.

Nominals with negative constructions will give you the following.

Yah thayekwatako' thiken' yeksa'a.
    [Yah t-ha-ye-kwa-tá:-ko' thí:-ken' yek-sá:-'ah]
        That girl won't / wouldn't fix (it).

Yah thayehninonh kiken' àthere ne sa'nihstenha.
    Yah t-ha-yeh-ní:-nonh kí:-ken' à:-t-he-reh ne sa'-nihs-tén-ha']
        Your mother won't / wouldn't buy this basket.

Yah tehotinenhskwenh ne kàsere' thiken' rononkwe.
    [Yah te-ho-ti-nénhs-kwenh ne kà:-se-re' thí:-ken' ro-nó:-kwe']
        Those men have not stolen / did not steal the car.

NOTE: The Negative construction is rarely ever used with the Future modal *en-*. When it does occur it is usually in response to a direct translation from English. It may be said, for the most part, that it is culturally inappropriate to negate the future since we do not know precisely how the future will be. It would be therefore *presumptious* to make negative statements about something that has not yet happened.

USING the HABITUAL PAST

The Habitual Past occurs as a suffix attached to the verb. When it is used a sense of *used to* is created. This suffix usually only occurs with the Imperfect ending on verbs: ie. *-s* or *-ha'*. It will then appear as: *-skwe'* or *-hahkwe'* depending upon the verb used by the speaker.

WITH ENDING: *-S*

Khninonskwe'. [K-hní:-nons-kwe'] *I used to buy.*

Kyenthoskwe'. [Kyént-hos-kwe'] *I used to plant.*

Royo'ten'skwe' [Ro-yó'-ten's-kwe'] *He used to work.*

Rontoratskwe'. [Ron-tó:-rats-kwe'] *They used to hunt.*

WITH ENDING: *-HA'*

Yakwatsthahkwe'. [Ya-Kwátst-hah-kwe'] *They & I used to use it.*

Saterennothahkwe'. [Sa-te-ren-nót-hah-kwe'] *You used to sing.*

Tekenonnyahkwahkwe'. [Te-ke-non-nyáh-kwah-kwe']
I used to dance.

Sometimes the Habitual Past suffix is used with States (expressions of being). When this happens the interpretation will occur as *was*.

Wakata'karitehkwe'. [Wa-ka-ta'-ka-rí:-teh-kwe']
I was well.

Wakenonhwaktanihahkwe'. [Wa-ke-non-hwak-ta-ní-hah-kwe']
I was sick.

Wake'nikonhraksenhahkwe'. [Wa-ke'-ni-kon-hrak-sén-hah-kwe']
I was sad.

USING the PROGRESSIVE

When the speaker indicates that the activity, action, or process in question is *going along* or *...right along*, the Progressive Suffix suffix -*hatye'* is used in conjunction with Objective pronominals.

Rotoratonhatye'. [Ro-to-ra-ton-há-tye'] *He is going along hunting.*

Yakohninonhatye'. [Ya-koh-ni-non-há-tye'] *She is buying right along.*

Yonkwahyatonhatye'. [Yon-kwa-hya-ton-há-tye']
We are writing right along.

Rotinenhstayenthonhatye'. [Ro-ti-nenhs-ta-yent-hon-há-tye']
They are planting corn right along.

The PROGRESSIVE with MODALS
Unlike the Habitual past, the Progressive can be used in conjunction with the Modals: *wa'-*, *en-*, and *a-*. The resulting constructions will provide the following interpretations:

WITH AORIST: *WA'-*

Wahotoratonhatye'. [Wa-ho-to-ra-ton-há-tye']
He was hunting (right along).

Wa'akohninonhatye'. [Wa'-a-koh-ni-non-há-tye']
She was buying (right along).

WITH FUTURE: *EN-*

Enyonkwahyatonhatye'. [En-yon-kwa-hya-ton-há-tye']
We will be writing (right along).

WITH NON-DEFINITE: *A-*

Ahotinenhstayenthonhatye'. [A-ho-ti-nenhs-ta-yent-hon-há-tye']
They would be planting corn (right along).

OWENNAHSON'A

VERB LISTINGS for further study: On the following pages is a listing 87 verb phrases (verbs with 1ˢᵗ person singular pronominals) as they occur with Subjective pronominals with Imperfect ending, Aorist with Punctual ending, and the Objective pronominals with Perfect ending. Using what you have learned so far in this text use these verb phrases to create new sentences. Remember the rules for attaching the appropriate pronominals: ie. remove the pronominal ik-, k-, ke-, wak-, or wake-, and then attach either the C-Stem or A-Stem pronominals depending upon the letter of the verb root.

---

ikhawe' [ík-ha-we'] *I have / carry (on myself)*; **wàkhawe'** [wà:-k-ha-we'] *I carried on myself*; **wakhaweh** [wák-ha-weh] *I have carried / did carry on myself*. With nominals: **ikhyatonhserenhawe'** [ik-hya-tonh-se-rén-ha-we'] *I am carrying a book*; **iktsi'tsyenhawe'** [ik-tsi'-tsyén-ha-we'] *I am carrying flowers*.

ikhserohen [ik-hse-ró-hen'] *I am ugly, ill-tempered*; **ikhserohenhne'** [ik-se-ro-hénh-ne'] *I was ugly, ill-tempered*; **enkhserohenke'** [enk-hse-ró-hen'ke'] *I will be ugly, ill-tempered*; **akhserohenke'** [ak-hse-ró-hen'ke'] *I would be ugly, ill-tempered*;

ikkens [ík-kens] *I see*; **wàkken'** [wà:-k-ken'] *I saw*: ie. **Erhar wàkken'** [Ér-har wà:-k-ken'] *I saw a dog*; **wakkenh** [wák-kenh] *I did see / have seen*: ie. **Onen wakkenh** [Ó-nenh wák-kenh] *I have already seen (it)*; **Yah tewakkenh** [yah te-wák-kenh] *I didn't see (it)*.

ikkwatakwas [ik-kwa-tá-kwas] *I fix s.t. up*; **wa'kkwatako'** [wa'-k-kwa-tá:-ko'] *I fixed it*; **wakkwatakwenh** [wak-kwa-tá-kwenh] *I have fixed / did fix it*; **Yah tewakkwatakwenh** [yah te-wak-kwa-tá-kwenh] *I didn't fix it*;

ikkwètarons [ik-kwè:-ta-rons] *I cut a slice (of something)*; **wa'kkwètare'** [wa'-k-kwè:-ta-re'] *I sliced it*; **wakkwètaronh** [wak-kwè:-ta-ronh] *I have cut / did cut a slice*; **ikkwe'taronnyon'** [ik-kwe'-ta-rón-nyon'] *I am slicing (cutting slices) it up*. See also: **kena'tarakwètarons** [ke-na'-ta-ra-kwè:-ta-rons] *I cut a slice of bread*; **kena'tarakwe'taronnyon'** [ke-na'-ta-ra-kwe'-ta-rón-nyon'] *I am slicing bread*.

ikyens [ík-yens] *I set, lay, put s.t. down*; **wàkyen'** [wà:-kyen'] *I set, laid, put something down*: ie. **Ohson'karàke yàkyen'** [Oh-son'-ka-rà:-keh yà:-kyen'] *I laid something down (there) on the floor*; **wakyenh** [wák-yenh] *I have set, put / did set, put something down*: ie. **Yah thiyewakyenh** [Yah thi-ye-wák-yenh] *I didn't put, set it down*.

---

kahronkas [ka-hrón:-kas] *I hear (of something);* **wa'kàronke'** [wa'-kà:-ron-ke'] *I heard (of something);* **wakahronkenh** [wa-ka-hrón:-kenh] *I have heard / did hear (of something).* ie. **Wa'kàronke' tsi tontàre'.** [Wa'-kà:-ron-ke' tsi ton-tà:-re'] *I heard that he came back.*

kahsehtha' [kah-séht-ha'] *I hide something;* **wa'kahsehte'** [wa'-káh-seh-te'] *I hid something;* **wakahsehtonh**[wa-kah-séh-tonh] *I have hidden / did hide something.*

kahtentyes [kah-tén-tyes] *I leave / depart;* **wa'kahtenti'** [wa'-kah-tén:-ti'] *I left / departed;* **wakahtentyonh** [wa-kah-tén-tyonh] *I have departed / did depart; I have left / did leave; I am away.*

katahsehtha' [ka-tah-séht-ha'] *I hide (myself);* **wa'katahsehte'** [wa-ka-táh-seh-teh] *I hid...;* **wakatahsehtonh** [wa-ka-tah-séh-tonh] *I have hid / did hide....*

kataterihonnyennis [ka-ta-te-ri-hon-nyén:-nis] *I read (to myself);* **wa'kataterihonnyen'** [wa'-ka-ta-te-ri-hón:-nyen'] *I read...;* **wakataterihonnyennih** [wa-ka-ta-te-ri-hon-nyén:-nih] *I did read / have read....*

katatis [ka-tá:-tis] *I speak / talk;* **wa'katati'** [wa'-ka-tá:-ti'] *I spoke;* **wakatatih** [wa-ka-tá:-tih] *I have spoken / did speak.*

katawenhs [ka-tá:-wenhs] *I swim;* **wa'katawen'** [wa'-ka-tá:-wen'] *I swam;* **wakatawenhonh** [wa-ka-ta-wén-honh] *I have swum / did swim.*

katekhonnis [ka-tek-hón:-nis] *I eat (what I've cooked);* **wa'katekhonni'** [wa'-ka-tek-hón:-ni'] *I ate...;* **wakatekhonnih** [wa-ka-tek-hón:-nih] *I have eaten / did eat...; I am eating.*

katekwas [ka-té-kwas] *I run away;* **wa'kateko'** [wa'-ka-té:-koh] *I ran away;* **wakatekwenh** [wa-ka-té-kwenh] *I have run away / did run away.*

katenhninons [ka-tenh-ní:-nons] *I sell;* **wa'katenhninon'** [wa'-ka-tenh-ní:-non'] *I sold;* **wakatenhninonh** [wa-ka-tenh-ní:-nonh] *I have sold / did sell.*

katerakwas [ka-te-rá-kwas] *I keep;* **wa'katerako'** [wa'-ka-te-rá:-ko'] *I kept;* **wakaterakwenh** [wa-ka-te-rá-kwenh] *I have kept / did keep.*

katerennotha' [ka-te-ren-nót-ha'] *I sing;* **wa'katerennoten'** [wa'-ka-te-ren-nó:-ten'] *I sang;* **wakaterennoteh** [wa-ka-te-rén:-no-teh] *I have sung / did sing.*

katerihwayenhstha' [ka-te-ri-hwa-yénhst-ha'] *I study;* **wa'katerihwayenhste'** [wa'-ka-te- ñ:-wa-yenhs-te'] *I studied;* **wakaterihwayenhstonh** [wa-ka-te-rih-wa-yénhst-ha'] *I have studied / did study.*

kateriyos [ka-te-rí:-yos] *I fight;* **wa'kateriyo'** [wa'-ka-te-rí:-yo'] *I fought;*

wakateriyoh [wa-ka-te-rí:-yoh] *I have fought / did fight; I am fighting.*

kateweyenhstha' [ka-te-we-yénhst-ha'] *I practice;* **wa'kateweyenhste'** [wa'-ka-té:-we-yenhs-te'] *I practiced;* **wakateweyenhstonh** [wa-ka-te-we-yénhs-tonh] *I have studied / did study.*

katkahthos [kat-káh-t-hos] *I see / look;* **wa'katkahtho'** [wa'-kat-káht-ho'] *I saw; looked;* **wakatkahthonh** [wa-kat-káht-honh] *I did see / have seen; I have looked / did look.*

katkawas [kat-ká:-was] *I quit / let go of;* **wa'katkawe'** [wa'-kát-ka-we'] *I quit / let go;* **wakatkawenh** [wa-kat-ká:-wenh] *I have quit / did quit; I have let go of / did let go of.*

katketskwas [kat-kéts-kwas] *I get up;* **wa'katketsko'** [wa'-kat-kéts-ko'] *I got up;* **wakatketskwenh** [wa-kat-kéts-kwenh] *I have gotten up / I did get up.*

katorats [ka-tó:-rats] *I hunt;* **wa'katorate'** [wa'-ka-tó:-ra-te'] *I hunted;* **wakatoratonh** [wa-ka-to-rá:-tonh] *I have hunted / did hunt.*

katoris [ka-tó:-ris] *I drive;* **wa'katori'** [wa'-ka-tó:-ri'] *I drove;* **wakatorih** [wa-ka-tó:-rih] *I have driven / did drive.*

katstha' [káts-t-ha'] *I use / make use of;* **wàkatste'** [wà:-kats-te'] *I used;* **wakatstonh** [wa-káts-tonh] *I have used / I did use; I am using.*

katyens [ká-tyens] *I sit down;* **wa'katyen'** [wa'-ká-tyen'] *I sat down;* **wakatyenh** [wa-ká-tyenh] *I have sat down / I did sit down.*

ke'nikhons [ke'-ník-hons] *I sew / mend;* **wa'ke'nikhon'** [wa'-ke'-ník-hon'] *I sewed; wake'nikhonhonh* [wa-ke'-nik-hón:-'onh] *I have sewed; did sew.*

kekhonnis [kek-hón:-nis] *I cook;* **kekhonni'** [kek-hón:-ni'] *I am cooking;* **wa'kekhonni'** [wa'-kek-hón:-ni'] *I cooked;* **wakekhonnih** [wa-kek-hón:-nih] *I have cooked / did cook.*

kenenhskwas [ke-nénhs-kwas] *I steal;* **wa'kenenhsko'** [wa'-ke-nénhs-ko'] *I stole;* **wakenenhskwenh** [wa-ke-nénhs-kwenh] *I have stolen / did steal.*

kenhotonkwas [ke-n-ho-tón-kwas] *I open (a door);* **wa'kenhotonko'** [wa'-ke-n-ho-tón:-ko'] *I opened (a door);* **wakenhotonkwenh** [wa-ke-n-ho-tón-kwenh] *I have opened / did open....*

kenhotons [ke-n-hó:-tons] *I close (a door);* **wa'kenhoton'** [wa'-ke-n-hó:-ton'] *I closed (a door);* **wakenhotonh** [wa-ke-n-hó:-ton'] *I have closed / did close....*

kenohares [ke-nó-ha-res] *I wash (s.t.);* **kenonhare'** [ke-nó-ha-re'] *I am washing...;*

wa'kenohare' [wa'-ke-nó-ha-re'] / *washed...;* **wakenonhareh** [wa-ke-nó-ha-reh] / *have washed... / did wash....*

kenònwe's [ke-nòn:-we's] / *like;* **wa'kenònwene'** [wa'-ke-nòn:-we'-ne'] / *liked;* **wakenonhwe'onh** [wa-ke-non-hwé-'onh] / *have liked / I did like.*

kerahstha' [ke-ráhst-ha'] / *draw;* **wàkerahste'** [wà:-ke-rahs-te'] / *drew;* **wakerahstonh** [wa-ke-ráhs-tonh] / *have drawn / I did draw.*

kerakwas [ke-rá-kwas] / *choose;* **wa'kerako'** [wa'-ke-rá:-ko'] / *chose;* **wakerakwenh** [wa-ke-rá-kwenh] / *have chosen / did choose.*

kerennha's [ke-rénn-ha's] / *get used to;* **wa'kerennhane'** [wa'-ke-rénn-ha'-ne'] / *got used to;* **wakerennha'onh** [wa-ke-renn-há:-'onh] / *'ve gotten used; I'm used to.*

kerhòroks [ker-hò:-roks] / *cover something;* **wa'kerhòroke'** [wa'-ker-hò:-ro-ke'] / *covered...;* **wakerhòronh** [wa-ker-hò:-ronh] / *have covered / did cover....*

kerios [ké-ri-ohs] / *kill something;* **wa'kerio'** [wa'-ké-ri-o'] / *killed something;* **wakerioh** [wa-ké-ri-oh] / *have killed / did kill something.*

keròroks [ke-rò:-roks] / *gather up;* **wa'keròroke'** [wa'-ke-rò:-ro-ke'] / *gathered up;* **wakeròronh** [wa-ke-rò:-ronh] / *have gathered / did gather up.*

ketshenryes [kets-hénr-yes] / *find;* **wa'ketshenri'** [wa'-kets-hén:-ri'] / *found;* **waketshenryonh** [wa-kets-hén-ryonh] / *have found / did find.*

kewennahnotha' [ke-wen-nah-nót-h a'] / *read (aloud);* **wa'kewennahnoten'** [wa'-ke-wen-nah-nó:-ten'] / *read (aloud);* **wakewennànoteh** [wa-ke-wen-nà:-no-teh] / *have read / did read (aloud).*

keweyentehta's [ke-we-yen-téh-ta's] / *learn;* **wa'keweyentehtane'** [wa'-ke-we-yen-téh-ta'-ne'] / *learned;* **wakeweyentehta'onh** [wa-ke-we-yen-teh-tá:-'onh] / *have learned / did learn.*

khehroris [k-heh-ró:-ris] / *tell her / them;* **wa'khehrori'** [wa'-k-heh-ró:-ri'] / *told her / them;* **khehrorih** [k-heh-ró:-rih] / *have told / did tell her / them.*

khekens [k-hé:-kens] / *see her / them;* **wa'kheken'** [wa'-k-hé:-ken'] / *saw her / them;* **khekenh** [k-hé:-kenh] / *i have seen / did see her / them.*

khena'tonnis [k-he-na'-tón:-nis] / *show her / them;* **wa'khena'tonhahse'** [wa'-k-he-na'-tón-hah-se'] / *showed her / them;* **khena'tonnih** [k-he-na'-tón:-nih] / *have shown / did show her / them.*

khenontens [k-he-nón:-tens] / *feed her / them;* **wa'khenonte'** [wa'-k-hé:-non-te'] /

fed her / them;   *khenontenh* [k-he-nón:-tenh] *I have fed / did feed her / them.*

khenònwe's [k-he-nòn:-we's] *I like her / them*;   *wa'khenònwene'* [wa'-k-he-nòn:-we'-ne'] *I liked her/them*;   *khenonhwe'onh* [k-he-non-hwé:-'onh] *I have liked / did like her / them.*

khenoronhkwa' [k-he-no-rónh-kwa'] *I love her / them*;   *khenoronhkwahkwe'* [k-he-no-rónh-kwah-kwe'] *I loved her / them*;   *enkhenoronhkwake'* [enk-he-no-rónh-kwa-ke'] *I will love her / them*;   *akhenoronhkwake'* [ak-he-no-rónh-kwa-ke'] *I would love / for me to love her / them.*

kheri'wanontonnis [k-he-ri'-wa-non-tón:-nis] *I ask her / them*;   *wa'kheri'wanontonhse'* [wa'-k-he-ri'-wa-nón:-tonh-se'] *I asked her / them*;   *kheri'wanontonnih* [k-he-ri'-wa-non-tón:-nih] *I have asked / did ask her / them.*

kherihonnyennis [k-he-ri-hon-nyén:-nis] *I teach her / them*;   *wa'kherihonnyen'* [wa'-k-he-ri-hón:-nyen'] *I taught her / them*;   *kherihonnyennih* [k-he-ri-hon-nyén:-nih] *I have taight / did teach her / them.*

kheyateròroks [khe-ya-te-rò:-roks] *I watch her / them (doing something)*;   *wa'kheyateròroke'* [wa'-k-he-ya-te-rò:-ro-ke'] *I watched her / them...*;   *kheyateròronh* [k-he-ya-te-rò:-ronh] *I have watched / did watch her / them....*

kheyawis [khe-yá:-wis] *I give her / them*;   *wa'kheyon'* [wa'-k-hé:-yon'] *I gave her / them*;   *kheyawih* [k-he-yá:-wih] *I have given / did give her / them.*

kheyenawa's [k-he-yé:-na-wa's] *I help them*;   *wa'kheyenawa'se'* [wa'-k-he-yé:-na-wa'-se'] *I helped her / them*;   *kheyenawàseh* [k-he-ye-na-wà:-seh] *I have helped / did help her / them.*

kheyenteri [khe-yen-té:-ri'] *I know her / them*;   *kheyenterihne'* [k-he-yen-te-ríh-ne'] *I knew her / them*;   *enkheyenterihake'* [enk-he-yen-te-rí-ha-ke'] *I will know her / them*;   *akheyenterihake'* [ak-he-yen-te-rí-ha-ke'] *I would know / for me to know her / them.*

khnekirha' [k-hne-kír-ha'] *I drink*;   *wa'khnekira* [wa'-k-hne-kì:-ra'] *I drank*;   *wakhnekirenh* [wak-hne-kì:-renh] *I have drank / did drink.*

khninons [k-hnì:-nons] *I buy*;   *wa'khninon'* [wa'-k-hnì:-non'] *I bought*;   *wakhninonh* [wak-hnì:-nonh] *I have bought / did buy.*

khyatons [k-hyá:-tons] *I write*;   *wa'kyaton'* [wa'-k-hyá:-ton'] *I wrote*;   *wakhyatonh* [wak-hyá:-tonh] *I have written / did write.*

kyenthokwas [kyent-hó-kwas] *I harvest*;   *wa'kyenthoko'* [wa'-kyent-hó:-ko'] *I harvested*;   *wakyenthokwenh* [wak-yent-hó-kwenh] *I have harvested / did*

---

harvest: ie. *kenenhstayenthokwas* [ke-nenhs-ta-yent-hó-kwas] *I harvest corn*; *ikhnenna'tayenthokwas* [ik-hnen-na'-ta-yent-hó-kwas] *I harvest potatoes.*

kyenthos [kyént-hos] *I plant*; *wa'kyentho'* [wa'-kyént-ho'] *I planted*; *wakyenthonh* [wak-yént-honh] *I have planted / did plant*: ie. *kenenhstayenthos* [ke-nenhs-ta-yént-hos] *I plant corn*; *ikhnenna'tayenthos* [ik-hnen-na'-ta-yént-hos] *I plant potatoes.*

tekahshenthos [te-kahs-hént-hos] *I cry / am crying*; *wa'tkahshentho'* [wa'-t-kahs-hént-ho'] *I cried*; *tewakahshenthonh* [te-wa-kahs-hént-honh] *I did cry / have cried.* ie. *Tohsa tehsahshentho* [Tóh-sa te-sahs-hént-ho] *Don't cry!* *Wa'tyonhshentho' ne takhenonke'.* [Wa'-tyonhs-hént-ho' ne tak-hé:-non-ke'] *She cried to be fed.*

tekatawenryehs [te-ka-ta-wén-ryehs] *I travel (about)*; *wa'tkatawenrye'* [wa'-t-ka-ta-wén-rye'] *I travelled*; *tewakatawenrye'onh* [te-wa-ka-ta-wen-ryé-honh] *I have travelled / did travel.*

tekatskàhonhs [te-kats-kà:-honhs] *I eat a meal*; *wa'tkatskàhon'* [wa'-t-kats-kà:-hon'] *I ate a meal*; *Tewakatskàhonh* [te-wa-kats-kà:-honh] *I have eaten / did eat; I am eating.*

tekenonnyahkwa' [te-ke-non-nyáh-kwa'] *I dance*; *wa'tkenonnyahkwe'* [wa'-t-ke-nón:-nyah-kwe'] *I danced*; *tewakenonnyahkwenh* [te-wa-ke-non-nyáh-kwenh] *I did dance / have danced; I am dancing.*

tekta's [ték-ta's] *I stand up / stop*; *wa'tektane'* [wa'-ték-ta'-ne'] *I stood up / stopped*; *tewakta'onh* [te-wak-tá:-'onh] *I have stood up / did stand up; have stopped / did stop; I am standing.*

tektenyes [tek-té-nyes] *I change*; *wa'tekteni'* [wa'-tek-té:-ni'] *I changed*; *tewaktenyonh* [te-wak-té-nyonh] *I have changed / did change*; Also: *tekattenyes* [te-kat-té-nyes] *I become changed.*

tekya'ks [té-kya'ks] *I cut in half / break in two*; *wa'tekya'ke'* [wa'-té-kya'-ke'] *I cut in two / broke in half*; *tewakyàkonh* [te-wa-kyà:-konh] *I have / did cut in two; I have broken / did break in half.*

tewakatonhwentsyoni [te-wa-ka-ton-hwen-tsyó:-nih] *I want / need*; *tewakatonhwentsyonihne'* [te-wa-ka-ton-hwen-tsyo-níh-ne'] *I wanted...*; *tenwakatonhwentsyonihake'* [ten-wa-ka-ton-hwen-tsyo-ní-ha-ke'] *I will be wanting...*; *taonkwatonhwenstyonihake'* [ta-on-kwa-ton-hwen-tsyo-ní-ha-ke'] *I would be / for me to be wanting....*

tewakhwihshenheyon [te-wak-hwihs-hen-hé:-yonh] *I am tired*;

---

tewakhwihshenheyonhne' [te-wak-hwihs-hen-he-yónh-ne'] / *was tired;*
tenwakhwihshenheyonh [ten-wak-hwihs-hen-hé:-yonh] / *will be tired;*
taonkhwihshenheyonh [ta-onk-hwihs-hen-hé:-yonh] / *would be tired / for me to
be tired.*

wakata'karite [wa-ka-ta'-ka-rí:-teh] / *am well;* *wakata'karitehkwe'* [wa-ka-ta'-ka-
rí:-teh-kwe'] / *was well;* *enwakata'kariteke'* [en-wa-ka-ta'-ka-rí:-te-ke'] / *will be
well;* *aonkwata'kariteke'* [a-on-kwa-ta'-ka-rí:-te-ke'] / *would be well / for me to
be well.*

wakatera'swiyo [wa-ka-te-ra'-swí:-yoh] / *am lucky / fortunate;*
wakatera'swiyohne' [wa-ka-te-ra'-swi-yóh-ne'] / *was lucky;*
enwakatera'swiyohake' [en-wa-ka-te-ra'-swi-yó-ha-ke'] / *will be lucky;*
aonkwatera'swiyohake' [a-on-kwa-te-ra'-swi-yó-ha-ke'] / *would be lucky / for me
to be lucky.*

wakateryèntare [wa-ka-ter-yèn:-ta-reh] / *know (about it);* *wakateryentarehkwe'*
[wa-ka-ter-yén:-ta-reh-kwe'] / *knew (about it);* *enwakateryentarake'* [en-wa-ka-
ter-yén:-ta-ra-ke'] / *will know (about it);* *aonkwateryentarake'* [a-on-kwa-ter-
yén:-ta-ra-ke'] / *would know / for me to know (about it).*

wakathonte [wa-ka-thón:-teh] / *hear (a sound);* *onkwathontene'* [on-kwat-hón:-
te'-ne'] / *heard...;* *wakathonte'onh* [wa-ka-thon-té:-'onh] / *I've heard / did hear..*

wakatkahritsheronni [wa-kat-ka-hrits-he-rón:-nih] / *am playing;*
wakatkahritsheronnihne' [wa-kat-ka-hrits-he-ron-níh-ne'] / *was playing;*
enwakatkahritsheronnihake' [en-wa-kat-ka-hrits-he-ron-ní-ha-ke'] / *will be
playing;* *aonkwatkahritsheronnihake'* [a-on-kwat-ka-hrits-he-ron-ní-ha-ke'] /
would be / for me to be playing;

wakatshennonni [wa-kats-hen-nón:-nih] / *am happy;* *wakatshennonnihahkwe'*
[wa-kats-hen-non-ní-hah-kwe'] / *was happy;* *enwakatshennonniheke'* [en-wa-
kats-hen-non-ní-he-ke'] / *will be happy;* *aonkwatshennonniheke'* [a-on-kwats-
hen-non-ní-he-ke'] / *would be / for me to be happy.*

wakatyes [wa-ká-tyes] / *throw (away);* *onkwati'* [on-kwá:-ti'] / *threw (away);*
wakatyonh [wa-ká-tyonh] / *have thrown / did throw (away):*
wakathenno'tsheratyes [wa-kat-hen-no'ts-he-rón-tyes] / *throw a ball;*
wakenhyontyes / *throw a stick.*

wake'nikonhrahseronni [wa-ke'-ni-kon-hrah-se-rón:-nih] / *am pleased (about it);*
wake'nikonhrahseronnihne' [wa-ke'-ni-kon-hrah-se-ron-níh-ne'] / *was pleased*

(about it); **enwake'nikonhrahseronnihake'** [wa-ke'-ni-kon-hrah-se-ron-ní-ha-ke'] */ will be pleased (about it)*; **aonke'nikonhrahseronnihake'** [a-on-ke'-ni-kon-hrah-se-ron-ní-ha-ke'] */ would be / for me to be pleased (about it)*;

wake'nikonhraksen [wa-ke'-ni-kon-hrák-senh] */ am sad*; **wake'nikonhraksenhne'** [wa-ke'-ni-kon-hrak-sénh-ne'] */ was sad*; **enwake'nikonhraksenhake'** [en-wa-ke'-ni-kon-hrak-sén-ha-ke'] */ will be sad*; **aonke'nikonhraksenhake'** [a-on-ke'-ni-kon-hrak-sén-ha-ke'] */ will be / for me to be sad*;

wake'nikonhrayenta's [wa-ke'-ni-kon-hra-yén:-ta's] */ understand*; **onke'nikonhrayentane'** [on-ke'-ni-kon-hra-yén:-ta'-ne'] */ understood*; **wake'nikonhrayenta'onh** [wa-ke'-ni-kon-hra-yen-tá:-'onh] */ did understand*.

wakena'khwen'onh [wa-ke-na'-k-hwén:-'onh] */ am angry*; **wakena'khwen'ònne'** [wa-ke-na'k-hwen'-òn:-ne'] */ was angry*; **enwakena'khwen'onh** [en-wa-ke-na'k-hwén:-'onh] */ will be angry*; **aonkena'khwen'onh** [a-on-ke-na'k-hwén:-'onh] */ would be / for me to be angry*.

wakenehrakwas [wa-ke-ne-hrá-kwas] */ am amazed / surprised*; **onkenehrako'** [on-ke-neh-hrá:-ko'] */ was amazed*; **wakenehrakwenh** [wa-ke-ne-hrá-kwenh] */ have been amazed*.

wakenonhwaktani [wa-ke-non-hwák-ta-nih] *I'm sick*; **wakenonhwaktanihahkwe'** [wa-ke-non-hwak-ta-ní-hah-kwe'] */ was sick*; **enwakenonhwaktaniheke'** [en-wa-ke-non-hwak-ta-ní-he-ke'] */ will be sick*; **aonkenonhwaktaniheke'** [a-on-ke-non-hwak-ta-ní-he-ke'] */ would be sick*.

wakenya'tathenhs [wa-ke-nya'-tát-henhs] */ am thirsty*; **onkenya'tathen'** [on-ke-nya'-tát-hen'] */ was thirsty*; **wakenya'tathenhonh** [wa-ke-nya'-tat-hén-honh] */ have been thirsty*.

wakyen' [wák-yen'] */ have*; **wakyentahkwe'** [wak-yén:-tah-kwe'] */ had*; **enwakyentake'** [en-wak-yén:-ta-ke'] */ will have*; **aonkyentake'** [a-onk-yén:-ta-ke'] */ would have / for me to have*.

wakyenta's [wak-yén:-ta's] */ acquire / get*; **onkyentane'** [onk-yén:-ta'-ne'] */ acquired / got*; **wakyenta'onh** [wak-yen-tá:-'onh] */ have acquired / did get*.

wakyo'te [wak-yó'-teh] */ am working*; **wakyo'tehkwe'** [wa-kyó'-teh-kwe'] */ was working*; **enwakyo'teke'** [en-wa-kyó'-te-ke'] */ will be working*; **aonkyo'teke'** [a-on-kyó-te-ke'] */ would be / for me to be working*.

* * *

CPSIA information can be obtained
at www.ICGtesting.com
Printed in the USA
BVOW08s0143060217
475374BV00001B/93/P